D1255231

Rethinking Architecture

At age thirty-four Carmen Anderson was in an automobile accident that left her paralyzed below the shoulders and also claimed the life of her husband. In Berkeley she found both a home and a community in which to raise her four young boys and to live an independent life, a large part of which was devoted to projects to benefit physically disabled and able-bodied people alike. Carmen was a great success with our students in the design studio and always opened her house to us. Through her we discovered what we needed to know in order to undertake the work described in this book.

In memory of Carmen Paz Anderson

a personification of *Independent Living* in
Berkeley and our first design consultant

Raymond Lifchez

Rethinking Architecture
Design Students and
Physically Disabled People

University of California Press
Berkeley   Los Angeles   London

University of California Press
Berkeley and Los Angeles, California

University of California Press, Ltd.
London, England

© 1987 by
The Regents of the University of California

Library of Congress Cataloging-in-Publication Data

Rethinking architecture.

Includes index.
Contents: Then and now / by Raymond Lifchez—Disability and the experi-
ence of architecture / by Cheryl Davis—An open letter to architects / by Cheryl
Davis and Raymond Lifchez—[etc.]
  1. Architecture and the physically handicapped—United States.
2. Architecture—Research—United States.
I. Lifchez, Raymond, 1932–
NA2545.P5R47   1987   720'.42'0973   86-7026
ISBN 0-520-04434-7 (alk. paper)

Printed in the United States of America
1 2 3 4 5 6 7 8 9

Contents

Foreword

Recently there has been an upsurge of criticism about the training of professionals in our society. Derek Bok wrote a compelling critique of the legal profession in 1983, and the next year he offered a provocative analysis of medical education. Others have noted serious deficiencies in the professional training of engineers, business executives, and educators. Throughout these critiques runs a common thread: As the professions become more technical and specialized the needs of clients tend to recede into the background. Some doctors, for example, seem to treat diseases rather than patients.

This book and the teaching program it describes suggest that a similar analysis should be applied to the architecture profession. By involving physically disabled design consultants in the education of fledgling architects, this curricular experiment provides a powerful model for how professional education can help students develop the interpersonal skills and empathy needed to best serve their clients. If we want our professionals to be more than technicians, our colleges and universities must devise curriculums that encourage students to view technical solutions—whether engineering products, medical treatments, legal decisions, or architectural designs—through the eyes of their clients. Only in this way will the next generation of professionals gain the necessary understanding of human variability and complexity.

Richard R. Johnson
Research Director
Exxon Education Foundation

Preface

Architecture is the thoughtful structuring of places to inhabit. It should be enabling. The architect should make it possible for people to have encounters with the environment that make them able to do more, to know more, to experience the world in ways that augment, rather than diminish, their sense of dignity and competence and joy, and that awaken their interest in one another. Architecture can do that: the light that enters a room and washes softly across walls all through the day; the outlook that brings evidence of the seasons and of judicious neighboring; the path that allows gracious movement between rooms indoors and out; the structure that allows choices between being enclosed and protected or enjoying outlook and exposure—all these add to the course of a day. They enable us to be more aware, more confidently a part of the world than we might otherwise be.

Imagine instead a place where movement is thwarted, outlook is denied, where nothing quite fits and the light is always either glaring or dim. These are the partial prisons in which many disabled people now find themselves. Architecture, properly cared for, can offer the opportunity to move more freely, to reach more easily, to see with less anxiety, or to enjoy a domain of touch and sounds and smells that expands the imagination.

Architecture can be enabling only if architects develop empathy—not just empathy for the way forces settle to the ground or for how the idealized body stands upright and intact like a column, but for the ways that architecture enters into the lives of people, people we know and love and others for whom we have not yet learned to care. This book is the story of an effort to make such a charge become an integral part of the study of architecture. It asks that we not allow the disabled to become the discarded.

Architectural education is a peculiar enterprise. Its primary goal is to educate people who will tend to the making of buildings that fit society. But society is an abstraction, its purposes vague, contradictory, and constantly in flux. Only in textbooks is society an entity. What architects do, rather, is to make specific buildings, in particular places, often for specific purposes and sometimes for specific people. At least that is what the contributors to this book and many of their peers think that architects would best do. In this they now face a counter trend.

Recently architects have become fond of looking for building types, categorizing the experience of many generations of builders into definitive generic forms that can give direction (and authority) to their own work. The proponents of building type argue that it is inefficient to "reinvent the wheel," that there is already a common store of patterns that provide perfectly good ways to make buildings, and that we need only understand them well in order to proceed. Further, they argue, the cultural memory of our society is embedded in these types and we abandon or ignore them at peril. They claim that such types, when used as guides to the production of architecture, will bring into the environment a rich set of resonances—memories and associations that have been collected around such forms in other settings—that will touch us all at some deep level. Types allow the organization of urban space within a larger framework: The consistencies of buildings all derived from a given type establish a basso continuo, as it were, for the melodies of the city.

But it is not often mentioned that many favor type solutions because they are easier to produce than are eccentric or intricate inventions that require the loving attention and patience of designers, builders, and clients alike. Nor is it often mentioned that typifying buildings makes them more predictable, easier to fit into the cash-flow and credit projections. Types, in short, are aids to recognition; they are useful to planners, developers, bankers, bureaucrats, and custodians, to those who have taken unto themselves the management of resources and who face many, often conflicting, pressures.

Types are of little use, though, to those who would know a building or a place intimately, to those who will live each day with the reality of the structure that a building sets down around their lives. Types can be inimical to those whose interests have not been served by a tradition of building that fits only the needs of dominant segments of society. Codification can institutionalize the neglect of minority concerns. The contributors to this volume are passionately dedicated to moving beyond the limits of type. They hold that architecture is specific, that it serves the purposes of individual inhabitants, that those purposes vary and cannot be arrived at by deduction. People differ, their needs differ, and those differences are not to be lightly swept aside in the interests of expediency. Rooms differ, and a room can change a life.

Two sets of people serve as the foci of *Rethinking Architecture:* a small group of physically disabled people and a group of students and teachers of architecture. In depicting an array of processes, aspirations, and tensions, this book maps an illuminating territory and reveals a world that cannot be contained by categorization. The lives of the disabled are shown to vary immensely, and the responses of students to new pressures and processes are shown to be extremely complex. Indeed, it is one of the central purposes of this book to show that, while disabilities may be categorized, the lived experiences of people cannot be reduced to generic types. Some of the people with whom this book is concerned have differences that dramatically affect their ways of interacting with the world by altering their perceptions, placing limits on their movements, or conditioning their means of communication. They are people who are confronting now, every day, circumstances that many of us will encounter for at least some part of our lives.

One of the most urgent messages of this book is the evidence it gives us of ways that society handicaps those who are exceptionally different in behavior or appearance or physical ability. Several of the authors give freely of their personal experience with disabilities and their feelings about encounters with physical arrangements that profoundly affected their lives. They are candid, too, about their anxiety that they will be stigmatized. They fear that with one set of abilities impaired they will be presumed to have few others. They know all too well the patterns of avoidance, the glances of aversion, the stratagems used by the able-bodied to deny, to put out of mind, the threat of a life that is circumscribed differently. They sense, perhaps, that the word *handicap* has come down to us from the language of seventeenth-century competitive games.

The students and faculty described in this book were participants in an experiment in architectural education at the University of California, Berkeley. As in all such efforts to intervene in a working system, the various participants had differing reasons for becoming involved in the project. A great virtue of the book is that it lets us hear the voices of many participants and to hear forthrightly conflicting accounts of what happened. In this it is true to its purpose: it shows us through its structure that the complexity of social experience does not reduce to a sum.

Readers who have not been a part of architectural education will perhaps be surprised by how large a part of the effort is taken up in organizational difficulties: organizing teams of students; establishing relationships between consultants, instructors, students, and clients; and clarifying objectives. (Those who have attempted to teach an unconventional studio course will appreciate the effort.) The studio, in which a number of students work closely with an instructor several days a week, usually on an individual basis, is a well-established cornerstone of architectural education. It pervades our thinking about curriculums and does much to determine the ethos of an architectural school and the expectations students have of their program. The studio can be a singularly effective means for bringing together knowledge, values, and action. Faculty who lead students through the processes of projecting new environments for people can entangle them simultaneously in the acquisition of new skills (and the languages that describe those skills), in confrontations with life circumstances and social values that are embedded in those environments, and in the difficult task of presuming to take action in an imperfectly defined context and within arbitrary time limits.

Obviously, the studio can be a potent forum for advancing a student's awareness as well as furthering the development of professional skills. But it can also (and all too often does) revert to the routinized production of emulative drawings, with all questions of purpose sheltered under the wing of a seductive professional elan. *Elan* is much favored by the architectural press these days, and therefore influential in the schools. Its attributes are more readily recognized in images of visual complexity than in descriptions of lived experience. The typifying image holds all its information at once, waiting to be deciphered or used as the springboard for private associations. To understand the experiences that a building actually conveys to its inhabitants, on the other hand, requires narrative descriptions that are sequential and are qualified by the context in which they happen. Such narratives demand sustained attention.

The stylistic image allows for simplistic identification; the "interesting" can too readily be sorted from the "mundane," the talented work from the plodding, the "good" from the "bad." When the attributes of the image become the paramount concern, when they serve as a basis for the most telling judgments, architecture withers. This book would instead have architecture expand and grow.

Donlyn Lyndon
Berkeley, California

Acknowledgments

Both this book and the work it reports on could not have been undertaken without the generosity of the Exxon Education Foundation and especially the goodwill and support of its research director, Dr. Richard R. Johnson. We are also indebted to the faculty of the Department of Architecture, University of California at Berkeley, who permitted us to carry out our special project within the framework of a "standard" course in architectural design. This was of great importance to our purpose, to introduce a professional concern for disabled people into the mainstream of architectural education.

Our effort to share the project with four other schools—the University of Cincinnati, the University of Florida at Gainesville, the University of Houston, and Kansas State University at Manhattan—yielded many important and unexpected insights. Of all those who shared in our work, Leland Shaw (University of Florida), W. Mike Martin (then at Kansas State University, now at California Polytechnic State University), and Dr. William Spencer (Baylor University Rehabilitation Hospital) made the most substantial contributions.

At the outset Anselm Strauss of the University of California at San Francisco illuminated the path from concept to implementation. Throughout the project we relied upon our board of advisors: Irving Kenneth Zola of the Department of Sociology at Brandeis University, Martha Ross Redden of the American Association for the Advancement of Science, and Nancy Crewe of the Department of Rehabilitation Medicine at the University of Minnesota.

The majority of the work was done at Berkeley, and we were supported and encouraged by a vast and diverse group of individuals there. The Center for Planning and Environmental Design Research at the College of Environmental Design sponsored us. Henry J. Lagorio and Sandy Hirshen, then the heads of the center, handled our finances and bailed us out of tight spots. Dana Cuff, now a professor at the University of Southern California, was then a graduate student employed to assist faculty members searching for funds by which to expand their research endeavors. Only with her able assistance were we able to successfully negotiate the lengthy grant-application process. Once Exxon awarded us a grant, we were in the good hands of the center's staff: Jaynet Tagami, Dale Tom, Bruce Miller, and Kellie Crockett, who looked after all the details in a most caring way. We also acknowledge a special debt to the late George Agron, FAIA, and to the many architects from the San Francisco Bay area who came regularly to our studio to take part in reviews and critiques.

We benefited from our many colleagues who taught Architecture 101, the course that was our vehicle. At the outset some were skeptical about the value of our project for undergraduate design students; but, on the whole, they were forbearing in their judgments and steadfast in their commitment to our purposes. Similarly, we acknowledge the social scientists who watched us and, in a certain way, watched over us. Their presence was a continuously steadying force.

In the center ring were our students and physically disabled design consultants. Over six academic quarters about three hundred students and twenty-seven disabled people took part at Berkeley alone. When I think back, I am still touched by their efforts and trust.

My wife, Judith Stronach, was a participant-in-the-wings. Few academic assignments are more labor-intensive than the architectural design studio, and this particular exercise in teaching and research was unusually demanding of my time. Her understanding saw us through those two years when it seemed to us that I was leading two entirely separate lives.

Finally, I and the other contributing authors to this volume express gratitude and admiration to our UC Press editors: Naomi Schneider, who sponsored the manuscript; Marilyn Schwartz, who saw it through production; and Amy Einsohn, who took charge of editing more than five hundred pages of reports into a final manuscript. As we worked on the manuscript and put together the pieces of our collage, I came to feel a closure to what had remained, despite our many well-earned successes, a somewhat personally troubling experience because of what it revealed about the deep roots of prejudice in our society.

The presence of disabled people in the design studio was intended to challenge students' assumptions about the people who would use the buildings they designed. In addition to confronting their own prejudices about disabled people, students were encouraged to consider all clients as complex individuals with specific needs, preferences, and dreams.

Introduction

Building forms reflect how a society feels about itself and the world it inhabits. A community's ideas, hopes, and fears can be read in the structures that line its streets. Valuable resources are given over to what is cherished—education, religion, commerce, family life, recreation—and tolerable symbols mask what is intolerable—illness, deviance, poverty, disability, old age. Although architects do not create these social categories, they play a key role in providing the physical framework in which the socially acceptable is celebrated and the unacceptable is confined and contained. Thus when any group that has been physically segregated or excluded protests its second-class status, its members are in effect challenging how architects practice their profession.

As Thomas Szasz, David J. Rothman, Michel Foucault, and others have argued, such institutions as asylums, prisons, and hospitals evolved in response to society's desire to remove "misfits" from the mainstream;[1] to a certain extent the nursing home, convalescent home, and sheltered workshop also serve

1. Thomas S. Szasz, *The Manufacture of Madness: A Comparative Study of the Inquisition and the Mental Health Movement* (New York: Harper & Row, 1970) and

this function. And the architecture of these buildings has evolved not in response to the needs of the residents but rather to meet the requirements of their managers, whose task is to control and protect the residents.

In the past twenty-five years disabled people have become among the most vocal groups to protest the ways in which our society has attempted to exclude them, and they have pointed to the architectural environment as the most obvious symbol of how the able-bodied population handicaps the disabled. Over time federal, state, and local legislative bodies have responded: so-called ugly laws have been repealed, and a host of ordinances, rules, and guidelines are now on the books mandating access and barrier-free design.[2]

In general, however, the architecture profession has followed behind the lawmakers, complying with applicable regulations but not exhibiting a hearty commitment to them, much less going beyond point-by-point compliance to envision new design methods and strategies that would serve the needs of all members of our society. Architects are not solely to blame in this matter. Conflicting and inadequate statutes, uninformed and disinterested clients, and a variety of social and economic factors all play a part.

But architects, it seems, have been more enthusiastic in adopting other types of new design criteria—energy-efficient siting or highly marketable condominium dwellings, for example—than in considering issues of accessibility. While no

---

The Age of Madness: The History of Involuntary Mental Hospitalization (New York: Anchor, 1973); David J. Rothman, *The Discovery of the Asylum: Social Order and Disorder in the New Republic* (Boston: Little, Brown, 1971); Michel Foucault, *Madness and Civilization: A History of Insanity in the Age of Reason*, trans. Richard Howard (New York: Vintage, 1973).

2. Until recently a broad variety of laws and regulations singled out physically disabled people for discriminatory treatment. Municipal "ugly laws," for example, barred disabled people from public places on the grounds that their presence was offensive and posed undue legal liabilities. A Chicago ordinance read: "No person who is diseased, maimed, mutilated or in any way deformed so as to be an unsightly or disgusting *object* or *improper person* to be allowed in or on the public ways or other public places in this city shall therein or thereupon expose himself to public view" (italics mine). For a survey of such legislation, see R. L. Burgdorf, Jr., and M. P. Burgdorf, "A History of Unequal Treatment: The Qualifications of Handicapped Persons as a 'Suspect Class' Under the Equal Protection Clause," *Santa Clara Lawyer* 15 (1976): 855, 861ff.

one denies the validity of access as an architectural concept, few professionals have had the vision to create new forms that are not inherently discriminatory. Furthermore, an emphasis on technical specifications alone simply transforms the disabled into impersonal objects, wheelchairs with a given turning radius. While specifications are important, they should serve as adjuncts to, not replacements for, an understanding of how disabled people can live independently in a world largely designed by and for the able-bodied.

Traditionally, schools of architecture have been the testing ground for new issues facing the profession. In that spirit, and with a grant from the Exxon Education Foundation, in 1979 I initiated at the University of California at Berkeley an experimental project called "Architectural Design with the Physically Disabled User in Mind." The goals of the project were to develop a reasoned critique of the traditional methods of teaching design, to propose and test alternative methods that would place clients at the heart of the design process, and to enable students to develop the skills needed to bridge the gap between able-bodied and disabled people. The project was intended to emphasize the theme of client accommodation and thereby to introduce the subject of disability into the mainstream of architectural education.

At the core of the traditional undergraduate curriculum in architecture is the studio course. There students form their first educated notions about the design process, which begins with meeting the client and concludes with the presentation of a two- or three-dimensional model of the proposed structure. Instructors of these studio courses typically invite outsiders to serve as technical consultants to the students and later to play the part of prospective clients. All the studio courses described in this book followed that time-honored practice, with two differences. First, our outside colleagues were people with physical disabilities, and they served as design consultants rather than as technical advisors; that is to say, we sought their opinions and suggestions on a broad variety of issues that, of course, included but was not limited to accessibility. The presence of disabled people in the classroom, we hoped, would challenge our students' assumptions about the people who would use the buildings they designed, induce our students to confront their prejudices about disabled people, and heighten their sensitivities to clients as complex individuals with specific needs, preferences, and dreams. Our second innovation was to require our students to create hypothetical clients for the buildings they were designing. We encouraged them to envision diverse casts—able-bodied and disabled, young and old, families and communities of friends, heterosexuals and homosexuals. This exercise compelled the students to imagine three-dimensional clients and to place them in realistic scenarios.

Between 1979 and 1981 some four hundred people—instructors, students, design consultants, and outside observers—took part in the project for various lengths of time. The original proposal called for five schools to participate for one or more terms, with our team at Berkeley responsible for pilot testing the curriculum and overseeing the activities at the other schools: the University of Cincinnati, the University of Florida at Gainesville, the University of Houston, and Kansas State University at Manhattan. (For reasons explained in chapter 5, however, we decided to discontinue the participation of the four other schools after a one-semester trial run.)

A few months before the project was to end, we began to think about the format of our final report. We quickly discarded the idea of producing a primer, a simple how-to book that would attempt to reduce our hard-earned knowledge and understanding to a precise set of fundamentals, for we had come to see that the process in which we had participated could not be so neatly encapsulated. More important, our varied professional approaches, which had been a strength in solving problems during the conduct of the courses, precluded an agreement on the content or structure of any such primer. It became clear that though we had worked together for almost two years we had each experienced the project in our own ways and had evaluated it by distinct personal and professional criteria.

We then decided that rather than mask our differences under the rubric of fundamentals, we would juxtapose our individual perceptions and interpretations, in the style of Vittorio De Sica's *La Ronde* or Akira Kurosawa's *Rashomon*. This book, therefore, is a collection of interdisciplinary discussions of the project. Chapters 1 through 4 present a set of personal and professional contexts for the project: the experiences of the project director and of one of the design consultants, the architecture profession's general approach to issues of access and client accommodation, and the project's pedagogical intentions and methods. Chapters 5 through 12 form a series of field reports from the perspectives of instructors, design consultants, outside observers, and students.

Readers will note some instances in which the authors repeat or contradict one another. We hope that these instances will give readers pause, that repetition be viewed as a form of emphasis, and apparent contradictions be accepted, at least tentatively, as a reflection of our divergent perspectives. But our differences are well offset by what we have shared—our personal and professional experiences with physically disabled individuals and our conviction that the relationship between architect and client is crucial to the satisfactory delivery of services. We believe that architecture students must be trained from the beginning to view their clients as partners in the design process through which ideas are fashioned into buildings. Perhaps more than any other profession, architecture requires an equal partnership between practitioner and client. We wanted our students to become convinced that their creative ability may come in large measure from the relationship they establish with their clients and that to inspire one's client may be the first step to achieving a well-designed building.

The dialogue between architect and client cannot be taken for granted. The goal of the dialogue is to discover the complexities of the client's life, dreams, and necessities—all of which are related to the architect's understanding of the design problem at hand. Talking with clients is an art whose rudiments, at least, can be taught. In our studio exercises we first asked our students to write biographies and scenarios for imaginary clients. Like authors creating characters for the story they want to tell, our students were to visualize clients for whom they would design. These character sketches and scripts were then critiqued by the instructors and design consultants. Our task here was to point out implicit assumptions that the aspiring architect needed to examine critically before moving on to the making of drawings or models. We were particularly alert to challenge stereotyped clients, especially one-dimensional views of clients who were physically disabled, elderly, or in other ways quite different from the students themselves. We wanted to be sure each architect created a client who possessed personal integrity and was clearly distinct from the student. When a student would, in response to a critique, defend his design by saying, "No, my client would not like that—it's not him," we knew that this student was beginning to develop an empathic understanding of his client, the prerequisite for a constructive professional relationship. (In a more advanced studio design course, the imaginary clients were replaced by real people, and the design consultants counseled the students on how to place the issue of access, as both a legal requirement and a humane concept, before able-bodied clients.)

A major hurdle for our students was to conceive of physically disabled people who lived normal lives in everyday society. For in the students' world view, consciously and unconsciously, the realm of the disabled is the institution—a misconception we took great pains to dispel and one boldly contradicted by the presence in the studio of our design consultants. Similar biases and prejudices against disabled people had to be confronted before our students could, with equanimity and imagination, realize that people who have physical disabilities are not a homogeneous mass defined solely or primarily by their disabilities. In the United States one of every seven persons in the noninstitutionalized population has either a permanent or a chronic disability. Some are children, some are elderly; some are single, some are married; some are parents; some are happy and healthy, some are not. Yet disability and disabled people are remote from most students' lives and are imagined to have shadowy, forbidding qualities from which students turn in discomfort if not fear.

We addressed this problem head on by requiring that one of the student's clients, a resident in the multifamily dwelling or a resident's close friend and frequent visitor, have a motor impairment. By having to place a person whose mobility is limited into a group of able-bodied people, our students were led to consider how to design an environment that would meet the needs of all.

To stimulate their imagination, we also encouraged students to turn to literature. Unfortunately, most literary works, both fiction and nonfiction, tend to link disability either to pathology (Victor Hugo's *Hunchback of Notre Dame*) or to extraordinary heroism (Helen Keller's *Story of My Life*). One is somewhat hard pressed to find descriptions of disabled persons whose psyches or souls are neither perverse nor saintly. Three autobiographies that were particularly effective in our course—in part because they were written by young men whose lives before they suffered traumatic accidents closely paralleled most of our students' lives—were Richard P. Brickner's *The Broken Year* and *My Second Twenty Years* and Ron Kovic's *Born on the Fourth of July*.

The initial shock students experienced upon finding physically disabled people in their classroom was both unavoidable and immensely valuable. Immediately they were jarred into a new and more complex perception of reality: The world is filled with a broader variety of people than they may have ever noticed. Our physically disabled design consultants were highly articulate about which particular aspects of an environment worked or did not work for them. Having spent their lives, either from birth or from the onset of their disabling condition, negotiating for the right to live normal independent lives in environments built without concern for them, they had become exceptionally knowledgeable about architecture, its social functions and significance as well as its physical forms.

The role we gave our design consultants in the introductory course was a tough one: They were to be consultants but not surrogate clients. Our students often tried hard, however, to turn the design consultants into clients, thus avoiding the responsibility of empathizing with an imaginary client by acquiescing to a flesh-and-blood person who, they hoped, would direct them toward the "right" solution. To avoid falling into this role, the consultants had to remain somewhat distant and had often to play devil's advocate. The design consultants also had to cope with a variety of insensitive actions and comments—from both students and instructors—during at least the early part of each term. Some students made it clear that they did not want to work with the more severely disabled consultants, whose speech was difficult to understand. Nor were the inhibitions and self-consciousness of the instructors insignificant.

The design consultants, however, were accustomed to being treated poorly by able-bodied strangers, and they had learned to take it upon themselves to bridge the distance others would enforce. Steve Hoffmann, who was born with cerebral palsy and uses a wheelchair, would break the ice with reluctant students by asking them to place their drawings or models on the floor. He would then slide out of his chair, sit or lie on the floor, and begin talking about the students' work. Students admired his nonchalant courage at being himself in public, and Steve became a great favorite.

Another consultant, Simon Brown, also had cerebral palsy and used a letter board and head wand to peck out words and phrases to students; usually an assistant accompanied him and served as "translator." Simon's muscle control was not as strong as Steve's; he often drooled, flailed his arms, and made unexpected sounds. Some students were attracted to him, others were alarmed, but all were too distracted initially to work with him. Simon offered students a "model" of how to relate to him by inviting to the studio several of his able-bodied housemates, a tight familylike group who worked as a team to engage the students. Sometimes this troupe arrived in costumes, as if to underscore that differences make people who and what they are.

Our project also benefited from the presence of outside observers, social scientists whom we contracted to evaluate our interpersonal and instructional processes. The outside observers attended studio sessions, interviewed a cross-section of participants, and administered psychometric questionnaires. We instructed them to keep all their observations and data confidential until the termination of the project unless, in their professional opinion, their direct intervention was necessary to prevent the project from seriously floundering. As it happened, just such an intervention proved essential to the project's survival during our very first term (see chapter 5), when we discovered that we had underestimated the interpersonal skills needed to carry off the project.

We began our project just as the long-neglected subject of access was becoming a pressing issue in public policy. Although federal and state laws now explicitly protect disabled citizens against various forms of discrimination in education, employment, transportation, and public housing (though not in private facilities), the biases and fears of able-bodied people remain largely intact. As is always the case with broad cultural prejudices, direct personal contact provides the key to dispelling stereotypes. By working side by side with physically disabled design consultants, our able-bodied students learned not only a valuable professional lesson about client accommodation but also a profound personal lesson about human vulnerability and humility.

Students constructed large-scale, three-dimensional models of their designs. Throughout the term, they rebuilt and refined these fully furnished, populated models as they became more knowledgeable about the complexities of making well-designed buildings that were also accessible.

1

Then and Now

Raymond Lifchez

Three or four years ago I met a young architect, recently graduated from school, who was working for a large New York firm
that had an excellent reputation in the design of high-rise public housing. She had been placed in charge of the design of a
regional library for the blind, and as I looked through her drawings I could immediately see that she had been well trained. I
asked her if she had enjoyed working with clients who were
blind—an interesting challenge even for a seasoned architect.
But no blind people had been consulted during the design process; neither the agency sponsoring the library nor her firm had
even considered involving any blind people in the project.
After all, she asked, what possible use could blind people have
been to her, an architect, in the design of a building they would
never see?

I was taken aback. I knew that her design concepts were not
as strong as they would have been had she talked with people
who had a firsthand knowledge of the experience of being
blind. And I knew that her assumption that the blind know
nothing of the physical world was completely wrong. Aloud,
I suggested that she had missed a great chance in not insisting

on extended contact with the library's blind staff members and some sight-impaired people representative of those who would use the library. She, and later her colleagues, listened with a certain disbelief. It was difficult for these well-trained, intelligent, highly skilled professionals to accept the idea that physically disabled laypeople might have something to tell them.

Fleshing Out the Phantoms

I, too, would once have wondered what use it was to an architect to consult with physically disabled laypeople. In the 1960s I was living on the East Coast, dividing my time between teaching and my architectural practice as a member of a New York firm; my work then included the design of psychiatric hospitals and schools for the developmentally disabled. Like most architecture instructors, I would assign my students design exercises derived from my own professional experience.

But I found it quite difficult to translate my work for so-called special populations into classroom exercises. Although I was sincerely committed to a humane vision of architecture as a discipline whose mandate was to address openly the special needs of the infirm, the elderly, the physically disabled, and similar groups, I had a nagging feeling that something about the exercises was not quite right, and eventually I sought other types of problems to assign in class. I rationalized my decision by saying that there was no way to relate the projects I cared about to my students' life experience, and that without a personal nexus they would have no basis upon which to make sound architectural judgments.

Only much more recently have I realized that my reluctance to have my students cut their teeth on these projects arose from my misgivings about the nature of the buildings that my clients—state agencies and public institutions—envisioned: Those hospitals and schools were essentially custodial structures to be designed for the convenience of the caretakers, not for the needs of the patients or pupils. Though I could not at the time have articulated my reasoning, my discomfort with this administrative paternalism had dissuaded me from using exercises in custodial problem solving to teach my students architecture.

When I came to teach at the University of California in the early 1970s, I discovered less archaic attitudes toward and assumptions about special populations. The political and social movements of the sixties (civil rights, deinstitutionalization and demedicalization, self-help and self-care) had also yielded a strong local "crip lib" movement.[1] In 1963 Ed Roberts, a severely disabled wheelchair user, had enrolled at Berkeley and was allowed to live in Cowell Hospital, an on-campus student health facility that offered twenty-four-hour orderly assistance. Several other severely disabled students, most in their mid-twenties, soon entered the Cowell residence program, and by the late sixties a core half-dozen, calling themselves the Rolling Quads, formed a group devoted to pioneering campus policy on disability and initiating university and community programs for the physically disabled.[2]

The town of Berkeley also had a sizable population of physically disabled people who were not students. They had formed several grass-roots organizations to promote the concept of independent (that is, noninstitutionalized) living and establish networks between institutionalized disabled people and those living outside. In 1972 several alumni of the Cowell program and others established the Center for Independent Living as a

1. For a brief history of the various social movements of the 1960s and 1970s as they pertain to physically disabled people's activism, see Gerben DeJong, *Environmental Accessibility and Independent Living Outcomes: Directions for Disability Policy and Research* (East Lansing: University Center for International Rehabilitation, Michigan State University, 1981), chap. 2.

2. At the disabled students' insistence, in 1975 the residential program was moved out of Cowell Hospital and into an undergraduate dormitory complex, where round-the-clock orderly assistance continues. Residency in the dorm is now permitted only during a student's first year on campus, when the new arrival can learn the ropes and file the paperwork to receive Social Security insurance, Medi-Cal, and services from the California State Department of Rehabilitation. The student is then in a position to hire attendants, purchase and maintain any special equipment, and begin apartment hunting. Over two hundred students have attended Berkeley through this program, and its two pioneers, Ed Roberts and John Hessler, went on to hold top positions in the State Department of Rehabilitation, where they helped to create independent living programs throughout California.

nonprofit corporation to provide such services as advocacy, peer counseling, referral, attendant care, and equipment repair for Berkeley's disabled residents.

Whereas my earlier professional contact with disabled people had always been channeled though a state agency, in Berkeley I found myself directly involved with the politically and socially active disabled community. In the few small projects I assisted with, I was overwhelmed by the difference between my earlier experience of having been told by able-bodied administrators *about* disabled people and now hearing these people speak about themselves, about their experiences, needs, and preferences.

This difference exerted a tremendous effect on my feelings about disability. Earlier, when I had worked on institutional projects, I had felt guilty and fearful in the presence of disabled people ("one accident and that could be me") and had viewed them as both emotionally and physically frail ("one mistake and I could offend or injure them"). In those days the disabled were phantom people who moved silently about in the background while I collected information about them from a bureaucratic third party. But once I began talking to individuals, each became a full-bodied person who engaged me directly, and my attention was quickly deflected from their disabled bodies to their fully able hearts and minds. I gradually felt less guilty, because I no longer looked away from them but faced them squarely and began to see them as they saw themselves.

I had feared I would discover tragic people because I had always seen tragic bodies. But that did not happen. Instead, the physically disabled people I met and worked with conveyed a certain strength and timeliness. They were certain (and were soon proven right) that their work was on the crest of a great wave about to break—the beginning of their liberation, through their own concerted effort, from centuries of social stigma. Though united in their protest at being considered second-class citizens, these individuals were an amazingly diverse lot who drew energy, purpose, and direction from their varied experiences. Blind, deaf, mute, paraplegic, quadriplegic; congenitally disabled and victims of traumatic accidents, progressive diseases, and chronic illnesses; teenagers, single adults, couples, parents, and grandparents; students, the employed, the underemployed, and the unemployed—they were all thinking people in the process of realizing themselves.

They were also excellent clients for an architect, for a primary requirement of the built environment should be to reinforce individuals' preferred image of their private and public selves, to set a stage, as it were, upon which human beings can have their highest ideals confirmed. I then began to understand why conventional institutions designed for special populations fail: They are based on the misinterpretation of the residents' or patients' genuine need for a dependent relationship as the need for custodial care, the provision of which juvenilizes the residents and patients.

Our society tends to place a high value on freedom, independence, and vigorous self-sufficiency. Any sort of helplessness is viewed with pity or scorn. But I discovered that one can define dependency less pejoratively and renegotiate the meaning of disability by redefining the loss of certain options as the acquisition of others. As Peter Trier once told me:

My being disabled is interesting insofar as it interacts with everything else I'm trying to do and be, and it poses interesting problems. But it's not interesting in and of itself. There is a certain range of things people ordinarily do for themselves that I can't do and others do for me. But then I can concentrate my time on things that interest me. In one way, my options are limited, but I probably have more time, energy, and focus for anything I want to do. Being disabled has caused me to make certain decisions about how to handle my life and time, but as a result I have done things and know certain people that I wouldn't have otherwise.

The more I talked to physically disabled people, the more I realized that a change in society's values and attitudes was the indispensable prerequisite to a barrier-free environment. Barrier-free advocates were not asking society to turn the environment into one giant appliance, filled with ramps and grab bars, but rather were asking communities to make a serious commitment to attention and caring. In caring communities, various mechanical fixtures would be perceived not as concessions to a minority population of disgruntled cripples, but as useful features in the community landscape, as symbols of its humanity, and as aids that would satisfy the needs of many constituencies: children, pregnant women, people carrying heavy loads, older people, and the temporarily disabled—both the unlucky weekend skier and the laborer injured on the job.

Architecture as a Social Art

The personal relationships I was developing and my work on a university committee appointed to improve access on the campus led me quite naturally to try to teach this new perspective of disability to my students. I began by asking them to think about disabled people when they designed their projects. To facilitate this work, I invited physically disabled people to visit the studio and talk informally with my students. A casual routine evolved. Someone would be invited to a review of the students' work or to give an informal presentation. If the students responded well, I would invite that person back to make informal rounds in the studio. This low-key presence kept the issue of access before the students and added a measure of a reality with which most students had had no experience.

From this experiment I began to realize how effective physically disabled laypeople could be as design consultants in the studio. Their anecdotal information about what aspects of the built environment worked for and against them, their sensitivity to physical and psychological barriers, and their inventiveness in overcoming those barriers showed quite clearly how much able-bodied architects take for granted about the environment. I also realized that their value as consultants was not limited to issues of access and barriers; rather, their presence offered students a moving and pointed example of why the design process had to begin with an understanding of the client and of how to acquire that understanding. The project Architectural Design with the Physically Disabled User in Mind developed from these insights.

"Too often, disabled people are expected to be experts on subjects such as ramps, and each is expected to act as a spokesperson for all disabled people. But what would be more useful to the student, I thought, was to describe the frustration of being unable to get to a terrific sale on lingerie or sporting equipment because the elevator was out of order, or the desire to find a wheelchair-accessible disco."—Cheryl Davis

2

Disability and the Experience of Architecture

Cheryl Davis

Cheryl Davis joined the Architectural Design with the Physically Disabled User in Mind project as an independent evaluator and later worked as a design consultant on the Berkeley campus. The following series of autobiographical vignettes exemplifies the deeply personal contribution the design consultants made to our students' understanding of the psychosocial aspects of disability. Our students could, in turn, realize that every client has a story and that part of their responsibility as architects would be to elicit that story.

My sensibility has been shaped by the experience of physical disability as much as by the society, economy, culture, and times in which I live. I could tell you the objective facts of my life, but they would tell you little about me; to truly know me you must try imaginatively to enter the realm of my subjective experience. For example, in the objective mode you would learn that I went to a special school; in the subjective mode you would learn how I felt every morning as the bus drove into the schoolyard, past a sign that read School for Crippled and Deformed Children. That sign stabbed me to the core five

days a week. It meant that society labeled me as different—
Other—that able-bodied people did not consider me a child
but a *deformed child*, and that I should be "happier with my
own kind."

When the study of disability is reduced to rehabilitative and
compensatory technologies—the planning of grab bars and
wide doorways—it becomes a subject of little human interest,
relegated to technicians. Unfortunately, social scientists—psychologists, sociologists, historians—have rarely regarded disability as a fertile subject for investigation. Yet physical disability is a *social idea* as much as it is an objective fact. (Imagine
limiting the study of women to gynecology, or the study of
racism to dermatology.)

A society's conception of what constitutes an appropriate
social niche for physically disabled people affects the demands
that a society places on those who design the built environment. The factitiousness of the environment and the concept
of disability are mutually interactive: The built environment
shapes the experience of physically disabled people, our self-
concepts, the way we relate to others, and our sense of our
place in the world. The environment is an arena where social
conflicts, often generated by the environment itself, are played
out.

The following vignettes may be painful to read; they were
painful to write. I offer them not to bare old wounds and battle
scars but to demonstrate the value of the subjective mode, best
entered through the analysis of experience, as a tool for understanding the interactive effects of society and the environment on the development of physically disabled individuals.

Living Upstairs

When I was seven years old, my family moved from Boston
to Milton, Massachusetts. Although the move coincided with
the great influx of southern blacks into Boston, our relocation
probably had less to do with that migratory phenomenon
known as "white flight" than with my physical disability. The
Jews of Cheney Street worried about their changing neighbor-

hood, but my parents' greatest fear was that as I grew older, and therefore heavier, they would one day soon be unable to carry me up and down the stairs. They had reason to worry.

Our apartment building lay more than halfway up Cheney, a steep slope leading to the summit of Elm Hill. Until I was three, we lived on the third floor. To reach our apartment, one climbed a full flight of exterior stairs and two more flights inside, about forty-five steps in all. My mother and father slung me over a hip, or sat me on a crooked arm, and then huffed and puffed the way up, a climb that left them increasingly weary and ill-tempered. I was always afraid of being dropped, and my consequent fretfulness annoyed them, as if, even so young, I was supposed to appreciate their efforts. After four years of this routine, when it was time to think about sending me to school, my parents must have realized that they could not carry me down every morning and up every afternoon five days a week (to say nothing of taking me on Saturdays to grandmother's house and on Sundays to Franklin Park). At that time we moved next door, where we would live for two years on the second floor. There, my parents had to contend with only four exterior steps and one flight inside—an improvement, relatively speaking.

For me, the move next door changed nothing. At an age when my peers were allowed to run downstairs to play with their friends, I depended on the willingness of my parents to "lug me up and down" (their phrase). When they carried me, I felt myself to be, in the most literal sense, a burden. I knew I tired them out, but I resented their fatigue when they groaned as if to demand that I admire their martyrdom. I had one flight less of complaining to listen to, but I was still a captive audience. Up and down the block, I saw children who were free, insofar as seven-year-olds are free. I was not.

After seven years of climbing hill and stair, my parents accepted the inevitable and we moved to Milton. After renting for two years, my parents decided to buy a home, and they took me along on some of the house-hunting expeditions. Their goal was to find a house they could easily carry me in and out of; they never talked about a house I could get in and out of by myself. (I am not sure they would have understood the difference between these two objectives.) Many of the houses seemed to my young eyes to be nothing *but* stairs. I looked at those stairs, and sensing that this was critical, made my opposition to these prospective homes as relevant to my parents' needs as I could manage. Thus I never pointed out that I could not get myself in and out; rather I reminded my mother of the last time she had strained her lower back carrying me up a flight of steps. The house they finally purchased was far from a model of accessibility (we didn't then know the word), but it was superior to several they had considered.

The new place on Houston Avenue was a two-family house, with a first-floor apartment six steps above grade. The lower unit had two bedrooms, which meant that if we occupied it my sister and I would have to share a room. Three years older than I, Karen wanted her privacy; on this she was quite vocal. The upstairs unit also offered access to several additional rooms in a finished attic. My sister could have a lot of privacy up there; I would have to crawl up yet another flight of stairs to invade her personal space. My parents explained the options as they saw them. Either we could have fewer steps for me (and less space for the family), or we could have "a few more steps" for me, lots more space for the family, and a bedroom for my sister. Then they said to me, "*You* decide."

I should decide? What was going on here? What were they asking of me? I was nine years old; who was I to say where we should live? If I chose the downstairs, they might go along but then forever complain and resent my having "made" them live in quarters too tight for comfort. Or they might not go along with my choice, and then I would see what I already suspected was the case: They had made the decision to live upstairs and were only pretending to give me a choice. I knew, though, that if I picked the upstairs, my parents would love me, congratulate each other for parenting such a "mature" child, and, most important, be able in good conscience to answer any future complaint I might make about the stairs with the response, "But the decision was *yours;* we gave you the choice." So with an air of "we only want what you want, dear," they ostensibly left it to me to determine where we would live. Feeling that I was being manipulated but unable at the time to explain how, and knowing that I had no real choice, I said that I wanted to live upstairs. They praised my maturity, and I knew that, in some important way, I had been had.

My parents tightened the bind in which they had placed me when they asked if I wanted a ramp up to the porch on the first floor. They pointed out that a ramp would enable me to wheel myself from the driveway to the level of the porch, some forty-two inches above. "Still," my mother added, almost as an afterthought, "you'll still have the flight inside to cope with, so it doesn't really offer so much, does it?"

"No," I thought, "but if we had occupied the lower-level apartment, it would have gotten me right inside." I knew what my parents wanted me to say. They reminded me how terribly expensive a ramp was, how hard my father worked, how little income the family had, and how much my last stint in the hospital had cost. Again, I made the "mature" decision, one I privately resented but for which I had ostensibly no cause to complain. After all, my choice had been freely made.

Leaving Home

I left home when I was twenty-two years old. I would like to say that my reasons for leaving were the same as any young adult's, but that would not be true. I wanted my independence, as everyone says, but what independence meant for me as a disabled woman was more than wanting to live closer to my job or having a social and sexual life unhindered by parents. (The absence of sexual activity was then so total that I regarded myself as nearly neuter.) I left because I feared the alternative: living with my aging parents, possibly for the rest of my life. I needed to find out whether or not I could take care of myself.

I had lived and quarreled with my parents in an inaccessible home, one I could neither leave nor enter. I could not afford a car; my father was always reminding me how expensive "under-twenty-five" insurance was, and he repeatedly said that he did not see how I could get a wheelchair in and out of a car by myself, despite my telling him that I had, in fact, done it. (It never occurred to anyone to equip the family car with hand controls.) Taxis were financially disastrous, and I could not maneuver my wheelchair onto a bus. I went places if and when my parents were willing to drive me; and they were willing to take me anywhere I wanted, as long as I wanted what they wanted.

My mother also believed that I could not minister to my own bowel care needs without her. She had convinced me too, for a long time, but I was beginning to question this. The idea that she might be mistaken was intensely disturbing. Did she need to feel needed so badly that she would sacrifice my independence? I was coming to resent her participation in my care as a gross and humiliating intrusion on my body, as an assault to my spirit. In the most basic physical sense, I had no privacy and I felt as if I were being repeatedly violated.

No, we did not get along. Our household was perpetually engaged in an undeclared civil war, and the hostilities would not end until someone moved out or died. Until I convinced myself that I might be able to live on my own, the only resolution I could see was suicide. I was beginning to think of it continually, and it terrified me. When I realized that anything had to be better than this, I finally found the courage to plan the move.

Eventually my parents realized that I was right; I had to move out. My relatives were astonished that they would "let me go," as if it were their duty to compel me to stay. In reminding them that I was a reasonably intelligent adult, my mother reminded herself. Before too long, my parents were helping me to look for an apartment.

As a low-income wheelchair user, my requirements for a dwelling were quite specific. The rent had to be $125 a month or less. The place had to be within a few blocks of Boston University, where I worked as a secretary, since I was determined to push to the office, except in bad weather, when I would have to pay for a cab. (Incidentally, cabs were very hard to get for such short runs, since the drivers thought that getting my wheelchair in and out was not adequately offset by the low fare. In winter, I would wait for up to an hour.) I had to be able to enter the apartment unaided and be able to maneuver in the kitchen and bathroom. Realtors would tell us only the size, location, and rent of vacant apartments. To find out more we had to run around to inspect each one, a colossal waste of time.

This was 1967, and most of the buildings in Boston's Back Bay were hopeless. None of them had accessible front entrances. Most landlords refused to rent to me, adding, "What the hell do you think I'm running, a nursing home?" Finally, Mr. Greenblatt rented me a basement studio near Kenmore Square and let my parents pay to have the back door ramped, "conditional upon the approval of the other tenants." Success! Let me describe this palatial abode.

To get to the rear entry, I had to push down an alley running between a nightclub-disco-bar and a movie theater. The alley, which had about a one-in-eight gradient, culminated in an expanse of fractured blacktop and loose dirt, deeply rutted and pocked by water-filled holes. I would never lose my fear of falling into them. I wasn't afraid of getting wet; I was petrified of being unable to get back into my chair in such an isolated spot, peopled only by enormous, sleek, and fearless Back Bay rats. In daylight they stood in your path and watched you approach, as if appraising your edibility. The route disgusted me, but it led to the only semiaffordable, partially accessible place I could find. In the absence of choice, I suspended judgment.

Inside, the studio was wood-paneled and dim. Some of the darkness was caused by the filth on the windows, the outsides of which were uncleanable because of the burglar screens bolted onto the frames. A front burner on the stove did not work, and since I could not reach the rear burners I had to cook one-dish meals until I was able to buy a hotplate. (Mr. Greenblatt never did repair the stove.) Although the bathroom door was wide enough, I had to remove it since it blocked access to the tub. That was all right for me, but I wondered if a doorless bathroom would disconcert any company I might have.

My parents gave me several pieces of furniture, dishes and

glassware, and their apprehensive blessings for the new venture. They moved in the furniture for me, cleaned the place up, and hired a carpenter to build a ramp, under which the rats soon made a fine home of their own. I could see that my parents were far from pleased with the place. I wondered if they thought I liked it or hated it. This, my first apartment, was small, dark, roach-infested, hard to get around in, and surrounded by an army of vermin. I loved it. It was *mine*. The door had a dead-bolt lock, and I could have all the privacy I wanted.

That first night, as my parents left me at my apartment, they assured me that I could call them any time of day or night. I had only to say the word and I could come home. I thought they were hoping my independence would be short-lived, but now I realize how anxious they must have been; I have seen the same pattern when disabled friends leave home. I must say, my mother could hardly have been reassured when I asked her, "How do you know when water's boiling?" To everything they said, I nodded and answered yes. Yes, yes, yes. They knew I could not wait for them to leave.

The next morning was Sunday. I awoke at nine and lay there on my bed, blissfully surveying my books, clothes, couch, walls, floor, ceiling, and door, luxuriating in my spendid squalor. I could let people in or out. I could buy the food I wanted, eat when I wanted, go to bed or stay up when I wanted, go out when I wanted. *I* would choose. I no longer had to come home early because my parents liked to go to bed early. I no longer had to ask my father to drive me anywhere. I could experience whatever presented itself, without asking my parents if it was all right with them. That was real independence. I thought of all that freedom and the new life I had begun. As I threw back the covers—I remember as if it were this morning—an incredibly wide grin streamed across my face.

At the Moscow Circus

I was excited to learn that the Moscow Circus was coming to Boston. Perhaps I was moved by nostalgia; many years ago

I had seen a pair of Russian dancing bears perform on the "Ed Sullivan Show" and I had never forgotten it. Besides, European circuses struck me as being much more fun than the three-ring American variety, which dazzled my eye but divided my attention. Whatever the reason, I was eager to go.

My life, at the time, revolved around disability. I was actively involved in several disability-rights organizations and working for a state agency on a program to develop housing for low-income disabled people. I wrote, advised, consulted, and did research on disability-related issues. Sometimes it seemed as if I did nothing else. I think I looked at the circus as a chance to get away from it all. This was going to be an offnight for disability. No axe-grinding, no politicking. I would go back to worrying about civil rights and human services later. For one lovely evening, though, it would be cotton candy and Pavlov's Performing Dogs.

A circus is best enjoyed in company, so I invited two friends, Kent and Marsha. Kent bought our tickets, advising the ticket office that one of us used a wheelchair and that we wanted to sit together. Once inside the Gardens, we went up several ramps and into an employees' elevator off the usual pedestrian path. My friends were shown their seats, which were several feet beneath the level of the aisle, while I remained in my wheelchair, since a transfer to the regular seat below was too difficult for me. With their heads at the same level as my footrests, conversation was awkward, but at least we were together.

The aisle, more than six feet wide, left plenty of room for people to pass me as long as I sat sideways. (My chair was less than twenty-three inches wide.) The arrangement offered uncomfortable viewing, but I was willing to put up with it. The management, unfortunately, was less willing to put up with me. The young usher, who sported a rather self-important air, advised me that "wheelchairs are supposed to sit over there," indicating a spot only slightly closer than Siberia.

"That's fine," I said, "but I'm with two friends who walk; they haven't brought their own chairs."

"You have to move. You're a fire hazard," he said.

"I'll move if you'll put folding chairs down there for my

friends." I thought that sounded reasonable, and Marsha and Kent seemed agreeable.

"Impossible!" he snapped. "I have other things to do."

"Then I'm afraid I can't move." I replied.

"Well," said the usher, "I'll let you stay, but the Chief Usher will be along soon. If you refuse to move for him, he'll throw you out. He won't be so nice." (I wasn't aware that *he* had been nice at all.)

Inevitably, the Chief Usher materialized, a red-nosed, pudgy man of about sixty. I observed him reprimanding young children a few rows below me. He enjoyed his authority as Chief Usher and he meant to use it. "You'll have to move," he fairly barked at me.

His bearing reminded me of my father. I suddenly felt tiny, vulnerable, and very young. I actually trembled. Then I stiffened, enraged that he should treat me in this way. Why the hell should I move? We paid for these seats. I was here with my friends and no one would separate us. "No," I quavered in a small voice.

The veins in his forehead popped out. His face was purely purple. He shouted. "I'm gonna get a policeman to throw you out," and left. I sat there shaking. My friends were angry yet calm, but I was intensely upset. They urged me to hold my ground and not permit him to bully me. Where did that usher think we were, Kent joked, Russia? Despite my friends' support, I found the situation hard to endure. The ushers were making me feel as if I had no right to see the circus with my able-bodied friends. They were wrong, I thought, wrong; but a small part of me was not so sure. For twelve years I had attended a special school where I could be with what they said was "my own kind." Maybe I really did not belong here.

While the Chief Usher summoned the law, I performed my own circus act in the stands. Dropping from my wheelchair to the floor, I crawled beneath the barrier, swung from it, and clambered up into a regular seat. Then I folded the wheelchair and brought it flush against the barrier. It now took up less than a foot of aisle space. Surely, I thought, the Chief Usher would be satisfied. I sat there regaining my breath, embarrassed at having had to crawl in public ("like a monkey," a relative used to say) but also feeling very capable. My improvisational use of the barrier to complete the transfer brought me some self-satisfaction. No sooner had I settled in than a policeman appeared. "That does it!" cried Marsha, "I'm calling my photographer friend at the *Boston Globe*." She and Kent sailed off in search of a telephone, leaving me alone with the law.

"Ma'am," he said softly, "I'm afraid you'll have to move the chair, or leave." He was respectfully courteous, and I resolved to respond in kind.

"I'm not willing to sit apart from my friends," I said, "but I may be willing to park the wheelchair elsewhere, if it's in a safe place."

"You can park it over there," he said, indicating an exposed area. Anyone could steal it there, I knew, and to leave my chair anywhere out of reach unless it were under lock and key was unthinkable and I told him so. "Why?" he asked gently.

"Would you leave your legs somewhere else?" I asked. "If my chair is stolen, I have no way of leaving this seat. It cost six hundred dollars, it's uninsured, and I can't afford a new one. I'm a working person; if it's stolen, the state won't get me another. Without it, I can't work, shop, make dinner—or leave the Gardens. Do you really want me to park it there?"

"But your chair is a fire hazard. You have to move."

I looked around us. From higher up in the stands, about twenty people dissatisfied with their seats had trickled down to sit in the aisles, on the stairs, anywhere they could. If anyone was creating a potential hazard, they were, not me. "If you make me move, Officer, that would be discrimination." He clucked his tongue and drummed his fingers, impatient and annoyed. "Do you see all those people sitting in the aisles?" I asked. He did. "Well, if you make me move, without making all of them move, that's discrimination."

Puffing out his cheeks, he lifted the bill of his cap, then expelled the air. Cheeks deflated, he looked depressed. "I'm sure not going to be the one to make you move," he said as he walked away. The Chief Usher returned just then, and so did my friends. The old man began to hector and bully me afresh. I had resisted all efforts to move for nearly an hour. The circus had been going on for half an hour and I hadn't seen any of it. I was tired, angry, and humiliated. Suddenly all I wanted to do was leave. Without even looking at the old man, who continued to shout, I told my friends I was tired and wanted to leave; did they mind?

As we rose from our seats, a little girl in a wheelchair entered, escorted by her mother and a girlfriend. She was crying, and from her mother's words, it was clear that she too had been told that she had to "sit with the wheelchairs," apart from her mother and friend. I was appalled. The little girl and I weren't the first people who had had trouble here. I remembered the experience of my friend Vivienne, who had come here with her five-year-old daughter. They had taken Viv's wheelchair away and forgotten to return it. As the Gardens were closed and cleaned up for the night, she had sat marooned in the stands for an hour, her child clinging to her in tears. The memory of that little girl in the wheelchair preyed upon me for a long time.

One more thing happened that night. On the way out Kent went to the ticket office to demand that our money be returned to us. He was advised that this performance was a fundraiser; no refunds were ever made for benefit performances. Where were the proceeds going? They went, Kent was told, to the Muscular Dystrophy Association, "to help the handicapped."

Can You Cook? If You Could, Would You?

Several years ago, I worked with a state agency to develop housing for the handicapped in connection with a publicly funded housing program for low-income people. We had identified a number of disabled people who were living in apartments maintained by different housing authorities, and we had obtained funds for a small program to make some of the most urgently necessary modifications to their units.

Our first tenant-clients were a married couple in their fifties. The man was able-bodied; the woman was able to stand with some difficulty but used a wheelchair nearly all the time. Aside from the steps at the front and back doors, the kitchen seemed to present the most glaring problems. We were prepared to modify the kitchen to make it fully suited to a wheelchair user if that was deemed desirable, but the woman quickly denied any need for modifications. We were disconcerted, yet my colleague seemed amenable to leaving it at that. I was not satisfied: If this woman did not want her kitchen made more accessible, there had to be some reason.

Taking her aside, I said, "We really want to do the best by you that we can, and we may not have the financial opportunity to do this again. I want to be sure that whatever we do or do not do is not based on a misunderstanding. Why don't you need an accessible kitchen?

"Oh," she explained, "my husband does all the cooking."

"And why," I asked, "does your husband do all the cooking?"

"Because I can't use the kitchen."

The circularity of this reasoning did not seem as obvious to her as it was to me, nor did its disclosure suffice to change her position. I changed the subject slightly.

"Do you *like* to cook?" I asked. "I mean, have you enjoyed cooking in the past?"

"Oh, yes!" she exclaimed, a distant glimmer of culinary nostalgia in her eyes.

"If you had a kitchen you could use, would you be interested in cooking?"

"Yes. If I could, I would love to!"

"Do you bake?" I asked, looking at the oven. She shook her head.

"Well," I said, "if the oven were raised, so that the shelf inside were about *here*" (indicating the height of roughly thirty-six inches), "do you think you could use it?"

"You mean you could do that?" she asked. I nodded.

"Oh!"

With a sense of the possible restored to her, the formerly reluctant client began to bubble over with information about her abilities, not just her disabilities. We quickly determined some of her dimensional requirements, the size of the space within which we had to work, and other factors. She seemed delighted.

As we left I was struck by the responsibility a designer bears for eliciting the necessary information from the client. The designer knows more about design than the client, while only the client knows how he or she lives. But the client may altogether lack any vision of what is possible; it is the designer who must be able to impart that vision, if only through suggestion. Only from a renewed sense of the possible can a client meaningfully participate in the design process. Thus, one should not ask, "Can you do x?" without also asking, "If we did y, could you then do x?" and, "If you could do x, would you want to?"

I also realized that we had asked both the woman and her husband about her needs, but not about his. He obviously cared very much for his wife and felt responsible for her welfare, and he had taken on the majority of tasks usually labeled "woman's work" (and in their milieu that label was unlikely to be questioned). I thought he might be unhappy to have to do all the things he did, but that having to do them made him feel needed. When we talked to him again, I glimpsed the possibility that he feared he might not be needed if we made all the changes we discussed. This apprehension appeared to make him unnecessarily resistant to the designers and their designs on his house. For him, we did two things. First, we left the work surface of some kitchen counters at a height suitable for him, tangible evidence that he still had a place in the kitchen. Second, we sighed from time to time about the changes in the house that we could not make because of spatial limitations, demonstrating that his role as a helper was still valid. We would never have learned anything about the husband and his needs had we stuck to our original intention of only measuring the lady and the kitchen, and we would have acquired a sea of postrenovation complaints for our efforts. We would then have defended ourselves by thinking our clients ungrateful and ignorant, when the fact would have been that we had not respected their needs or gotten to know them.

Although all our clients were disabled individuals and families with disabled members, the social and psychological aspects of their situations were astonishingly varied. Accessibility was the dominant issue that brought our team into the picture, but every time we found it necessary to consider the contextual matrix: family members' interests, cultural background, neighborhood resources, and interpersonal relationships.

To make a place accessible takes more than a ramp. Not only is a ramp not enough, at times one can be inappropriate, an indicator that siting issues may not have been resolved in the best manner. But the ramp has become a symbol of access in a way, so let us conclude simply that where it is necessary, it may not be sufficient. Attention must be focused on the way in which a physically disabled person is or is not supported by his surroundings and on how he experiences them. Understanding how a disabled person experiences architecture heightens the designer's sense of social responsibility. Designers who consider disability a factor apart from others, or who think it can be "figured in" subsequent to the "real" design process, do so at their own risk.

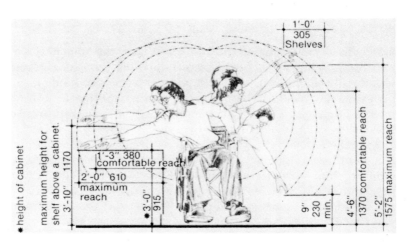

height of cabinet

maximum height for
shelf above a cabinet.

3'-10" 1170

1'-3" 380
comfortable reach

2'-0" 610
maximum
reach

3'-0" 915

9" 230 min.

4'-6" 1370 comfortable reach

5'-2" 1575 maximum reach

1'-0"
305
Shelves

An illustration, from a manual on barrier-free design, of the functional abilities of a seated paraplegic. Few designers, however, have the empathic knowledge necessary to translate this set of quantifiable factors into an environment that is both physically accessible and emotionally supportive. (State of Illinois, *Accessibility Standards, Illustrated* [Springfield, Ill.: Capital Development Board, June 1978])

3

An Open Letter to Architects

Cheryl Davis and Raymond Lifchez

In recent decades the conception of architecture as high art, as pure design, has become the banner under which many creative talents have sought new and daring architectural forms. By and large, the results have been buildings that do satisfy a range of human needs, although at times one senses that the architect unwisely sacrificed functional concerns for the sake of aesthetic vision and self-expression. Yet the question remains: How ethical is it to practice architecture—to be a professional licensed to design buildings and places of assembly—without having first developed an intellectual and emotional understanding of people?

Up until the late 1960s there was almost no public policy discussion in the United States about physical disability.[1] Most

1. The treatment accorded physically disabled people in the United States first became a somewhat public issue at the end of World War II, when various improvements in battlefield medicine produced a new class of veteran: "In World War I, only 400 men with wounds that paralyzed them from the waist down survived at all, and 90 percent of them died before they reached home. In World War II, 2,000 paraplegics lived and 1,700 of them are alive today [in 1967]" (*Design for All Americans* [Washington, D.C.: President's Committee on

physically disabled people were unable to move about independently—even had the environment been more sympathetic—and they lived as invalids at home, in hospitals, or in permanent-care institutions. Physically disabled people were not out in the world, and there was little reason to modify the environment to accommodate them.

Today the situation is very different. The number of people disabled by diseases of progressive age (heart conditions, hypertension, rheumatism, arthritis) is rising as life expectancies increase, and medical advances continue to lengthen the lifespans of those disabled by congenital diseases, illness, and accidents. Technology offers the physically disabled a range of aids and appurtenances that allow them to play more than the invalid's role, and the independent living movement has lobbied for the civil rights and benefit rights that support individuals' abilities to live in the least restrictive environment. Some thirty-two million Americans—15 percent of the noninstitutionalized population—have a sensory or motor impairment that interferes with basic activities such as walking, going outside, bathing, and dressing. About one-fourth of this group—eight million Americans—are considered severely disabled: children and adolescents unable to attend school and adults unable to work or keep house for themselves.[2]

Decade by decade the proportion of the population that is physically disabled is rising, and as the post-World War II baby-boom generation ages, the proportion will rise faster still.

Employment of the Handicapped, 1967], 5). To encourage the private sector to provide jobs for disabled veterans, Truman established the President's Committee on Employment of the Handicapped. Unfortunately, the committee's effort failed to take into account a host of relevant problems, including employers' attitudes toward the disabled, the veterans' need for vocational retraining appropriate to their disabilities, and the physical inaccessibility of workplaces and public transit.

2. Figures based on data collected by the National Center for Health Statistics in 1979 (the most recent year for which survey data are available). The survey also shows that of Americans age sixty-five or older, about one in four (29.1 percent) has a limiting disability and about one in seven in this age cohort (16.9 percent) is severely disabled. Also, between 1966 and 1976 the U.S. population increased by 10 percent, while the number of physically disabled Americans rose by 37 percent. For these and other demographic data, see Gerben DeJong and Raymond Lifchez, "Physical Disability and Public Policy," *Scientific American* 248, no. 6 (June 1983): 40–49.

Those among us who are able-bodied can no longer rationalize treating physically disabled people as "them," an alien minority. This is not simply a matter of humanitarian bonhomie, for "they" now includes our parents, siblings, and children, our friends, neighbors, and colleagues, and—one day—ourselves. The majority of disabled people in this country do not live in institutions and either do not have families to take care of them or do not want their families to do so. With moderate support services, many can live independently, and there is good economic reason for them to do so. Being out in the world, they need a world they can use. But the architecture profession has been slow to take note of the environmental implications of these demographic and socioeconomic changes and incorporate them into the mainstream of the profession's concerns. Although some architects have begun to awaken to their mandate, professional schools of architecture are still reluctant to teach a perspective of disability to their students, and most practitioners view access as a special interest or an afterthought.

The pulse of the profession in 1977, when federal regulations mandating access were first promulgated, was epitomized in a short article in the *San Francisco Bay Architect's Review*:

Protection of public safety and health keeps taking on an ever expanding definition. Can public codes really serve everyone's special needs and still be responsive to the general public's values? Provisions to help the handicapped trip the blind where the curb is cut away. The San Francisco State Student Union Building is forced to abandon altogether some spaces that were approved but were inaccessible to those in wheelchairs. What does this suggest for the fate of future preservation and reuse projects? Architects have used stairs as a design element through history and are we now to outlaw them even where they are integral in our buildings, if they are open to the public? *Let's hope that the success of the handicapped lobby doesn't inspire the hayfever sufferers to a similar program to require the defoliation of grass and trees in public open spaces* [my emphasis].[3]

3. Unsigned review, "The Handicapped Lobby," *San Francisco Bay Architects' Review*, May 1977, p. 6.

Clearly the word was out: If the physically disabled had their way, they would turn the world into one giant appliance with ramps and grab bars everywhere! What of course was not openly expressed was the fear that all those handicapped people who had stayed so nicely out of sight would now be free to compete for a place in the sun. How unseemly. And how uninspiring to the designer.

At the other end of the spectrum, when a client has unique requirements, can specify these needs, and can pay to have them met, architects take the challenge in stride. One of the most celebrated examples is a house designed by Charles Moore and Richard Oliver for a family of four, headed by a blind father. Here's part of Moore's description of his client and task:

[The father] while in his thirties has gone blind of retinitis pigmentosa. It's a small family but they are wealthy and had a beautiful site that they had bought before he was stricken. The fellow is extraordinary. He's still a famous skier and goes on shooting the slope considerably faster than other people do, listening to the yodel of his guide in the distance. . . . I've never watched this phenomenon, but everything he does is done with a kind of sureness and assertion and strength. . . . He had already, in the course of a very few years of being blind, learned to read Braille . . . had also gotten used to walking down the street and being able to know when there's a building there and when there isn't by the way the air feels on him, which, you can imagine, makes him extremely interested in how the air feels. No factory air for him . . . but rather the natural breezes with their variations and . . . the pleasure of a breeze in the summertime coming over you rather than just the constant nothing of seventy-two–degree air out of a machine. . . . We did manage to fix their house so that there's only about a week during the summer . . . it's in a hot area near here [New York City] . . . when the air conditioning has to be turned on. The architects he had talked to [before hiring Moore and Oliver] were interested in giving him an open plan because that's what modern architects give you . . . and what he did not need was a situation in which he didn't know who was in the room with him because he could hear voices from other places in the house. We gave him discrete rooms so that the acoustical environment in each one was complete. In order to get the sound right in those rooms, we had an interesting time of going, either with or without him, to a number of rooms where he felt particularly comfortable, including his sister-in-law's living room and a club in New York. It turned out that the rooms shared a number of qualities. They were high and some had stone walls and other rooms had balconies and bookshelves and projections and didn't bang in his ears.[4]

Everyone applauds such an empathic one-to-one relationship between architect and client. And it is worthwhile to note that the commission did not require Moore to learn new technical strategies but rather to explore new perceptions of the abilities of blind people ("shooting the slope") and their compensatory strategies (interpreting changes in air pressure and acoustics). This is not to disparage Moore's genius, but simply to say that well-trained architects usually have the technical knowledge they need to address the requirements of disabled clients; what many designers lack, however, is the subjective understanding of these clients' lives.

It is when all buildings are to be made barrier-free, when all disabilities are to be taken into account, when the client is Any Person (able-bodied and disabled, child and eighty-five-year-old), that architects usually find the charge overwhelming. Where does one begin? What assumptions can one make about needs? What questions are to be asked, and of whom? One feels as if one were suddenly being asked to rethink the entire history of Western architecture, in which the able-bodied have been the sole perceived users.

Most designers are familiar with various cookbook assertions that access to a building entails a ramp. The manuals dryly explain: "This is a ramp, and these are the specifications to follow for making one," but they do not advise how to make an intelligent decision about whether or not to use a ramp, what kind of ramp to use for a given structure on a given site, or how best to provide access to a given structure. For example, as a general rule an access ramp for a public building is preferably placed at the front, so that those who use the ramp may enter at the same place as others; but in a private home a ramp

4. Moore's comments were made at the Design for All People Conference, held in New York City on 22–24 January 1982. For reviews of the house, see "Extrasensory Perceptions," *Progressive Architecture*, April 1978, pp. 82–85; "Two Houses by Charles Moore," *Architectural Record*, June 1977, pp. 109–16.

invisible from the street may well be preferable, so as not to call attention to the increased vulnerability of the occupants.

For a designer these manuals are boring, lifeless, and, in a way, confusing. The designer finds them too prescriptive by far, yet they leave too much to his or her own discretion. This is fine if the designer has the empathic understanding and critical knowledge needed to exercise broad discretion, but few designers have refined sensitivities and skills in this area.

Accessibility as a Quality of Experience

Accessibility for able-bodied people refers to the degree of ease with which one can reach a destination. One may be able to drive to a downtown building but be unable to gain access to it if parking provisions are inadequate. So one decides to take the bus downtown, one enters the building, and that is that. But for a physically disabled person, getting there is only half the problem. For once there, he or she may or may not be able to enter easily, circulate through, and enjoy full use of the building or facility. In a factory, for example, a manager may be able to reach the administrative offices but not the assembly line. Or a student may be able to enter the classrooms but not gain access to the laboratory bench; a moviegoer may be able to see the film but unable to use the bathroom.

If a facility can accommodate the needs and wants of disabled people, allowing them not only to enter the place but also to experience it in a meaningful and reasonably comfortable fashion, then its designer has really achieved something. For accessibility is more than a matter of admittance or logistics; it is also a quality of experience. How one feels about a place, how one interprets it, or even whether one can adequately interpret it—these are all less quantifiable, but crucially important, aspects of accessibility. A place that supports people's activities and desires, permits them to be and do what they want, and causes them a minimum of pain, frustration, and embarrassment is more accessible than a place that confuses, harasses, or intimidates people. Many ostensibly accessible sites differ substantially in the quality of experience they offer.

Wheelchair access problems are the most obvious and pressing for the designer, particularly in the demands they place on dimensions and changes in level. But the environment is obviously not meant only for people in wheelchairs. What is optimal for the wheelchair user may not be optimal for the person who uses an artificial lower limb, and the needs of sensory-impaired people are yet more subtle. Broadly speaking, there are three kinds of disabilities: sensory distortions and deficits, motor impairments, and emotional and cognitive impairments. Each disabling condition requires a particular set of compensatory behaviors and activities, and an accessible environment is one that supports compensatory maneuvers.

Blind people, for example, depend on fixed landmarks for orientation and rely heavily on auditory perceptions and changes in air pressure; to a lesser degree, they also rely on olfactory sensations and temperature gradients. The blind person who has been mobility trained has learned to substitute these nonvisual inputs for visual ones in assembling an effective cognitive map. Inadequate compensatory cues not only prevent a blind person from moving from one spot to another but also prompt feelings of insecurity, annoyance, emotional and physical disorientation, and inadequacy. Environments that do not offer coherent nonvisual cues thus unnecessarily handicap the blind and create a psychological feedback loop: The disoriented blind person feels himself to be, and is perceived by others as, incapable, and this image of inability sustains the continued creation of a recalcitrant environment.

Similarly, a person whose hearing is impaired will compensate by developing a refined sensitivity to changes in light intensity and vibration (the conduction of sound through a wooden floor, touched object, and the human body). The vibratory conductivity of certain materials enables deaf people to dance and enjoy some types of music. For conversation deaf and severely hearing-impaired people learn to rely on visual cues. While the ambience created by low light may be romantic or relaxing for those with normal hearing, for a deaf person dim light jeopardizes conversation. Even those trained in and comfortable with sign language depend on facial expressions to convey subtle nuances. In a dimly lit room, the hearing-impaired are reduced to silence, polite smiles and nods, and frustrating bewilderment.

People with motor impairments have different needs still. A person in a wheelchair obviously requires aisle clearance and turning space, but height requirements are also crucial. Sitting in a wheelchair places a person higher than people sitting in regular chairs but lower than people who are standing. The seat of a wheelchair, especially with a cushion (essential for many people's health and comfort), may be three to seven inches higher than conventional seating, with the resulting difference in eye level tending to hinder rapport and intimacy. And since the eye level of a person seated in a wheelchair is at about that of a child, many people unconsciously tend to treat wheelchair users as children. High counters pose a special problem. At a bank a wheelchair user is often reduced to flailing his arms high above his head in order to attract the attention of a teller on the other side of the counter.

The design requirements for our third category of disabling conditions—emotional and cognitive impairments—are surely the most difficult challenge for architects. Whereas sensory and motor impairments pose environmental requirements that are not unusual (entry and exit, vertical and horizontal articulation, visibility, acoustics, and the like), emotional and cognitive impairments pose highly individual psychosocial desiderata. In such cases the designer must be ever more sensitive to his or her client's psychological traits, for the client may be able-bodied but dysfunctional in negotiating the everyday environment because of poor cognitive mapping, faulty memory, or extreme discomfort and disorientation in certain social situations or spatial configurations. Designers must therefore work closely with specialists who can identify special needs and judge the design before it is implemented.

Finally, the particular nature of an individual's disability creates a variety of environmental needs. Spinal cord injuries, for example, not only cause paralysis but also affect metabolism, the body's internal thermostat; as a result, some quadriplegics feel chilled when the room temperature falls below 75°F or 80°F, and they require housing that features thermostats in each room. And although the bathroom grab bar may have become one of the more visible emblems of accessibility, its use requires an upper-body strength and finger muscle control that is beyond the abilities of some paraplegics and all quadriplegics.

The Social and Psychological Matrix of Disability

Disability also exerts a broad variety of social and psychological effects. For example, a mobility-impaired adult living with two other adults does not absolutely have to be able to enter every bedroom in the house, as long as he can get into his own. But what if he is the parent of two children? If their rooms are upstairs, how does he supervise them, make sure they have picked up their toys, read them to sleep at night? In this case the inaccessibility of the upstairs bedrooms may seriously undermine his role and function as a responsible and caring father. Or consider the need of a disabled child to be with other children, to expand her competence, and to explore. These psychosocial needs clearly merit the designer's attention so that the child's disability will not overwhelm all the other aspects of her personal growth and cognitive development. Again, a purely logistical approach to accessibility is inadequate.

Though no one expects designers to become rehabilitation experts, there is one compensatory skill that designers can develop: the ability to elicit information relevant to the design process. Summoning a consultant, usually able-bodied, who is regarded as having expertise in dealing with "those people," is simply insufficient. Direct contact can, of course, be difficult, especially if the designer is uncomfortable talking to disabled people and especially when the questions that need to be asked are personal or intimate. So the designer needs to learn what to ask, how to ask, and what to do with the answers. All the while the design professional needs to remember that although the client may know more about the way he or she manages daily tasks, the client is probably no more an expert on disability than is the designer. A client's current performance may be but a shadow of what he or she could manage in a better-designed environment.

The designer may ask a disabled client, "Do you cook?" or, "Do you clean the house yourself?" and note the reply. But the design implications of the client's response cannot be determined until the designer finds out *why* the client does not do certain things without assistance and what that task means to the client. He may be physically unable to cook, or he may simply hate to cook, or he may think himself unable to cook because he does not realize how his kitchen could be modified to meet his needs, or perhaps someone else in the household has taken the kitchen over as a personal realm. None of these explanations, however, will be elicited by the question "Do you cook?"; "Can you cook?" is similarly insufficient.

Simply put, yes/no questions cannot serve as a basis for design, and a designer cannot count on the client's being able to express meaningful design requirements on demand. Such explicitness is not within the average client's domain of expertise, disabled or not—it is the designer who is assumed to have the necessary skills. A designer, by virtue of training, should be able to envision the hypothetical possibilities for improvement and be willing to explore some of them with the client. Designer and client must work together to see things not only as they are and to ask why, but to see things as they are not and ask why not.

Gaining Awareness

Architects thus need to acquire insight into the social and psychological dimensions of the relationships between physically disabled people and the built environment. One way to do so is, quite simply, for architects to talk with a variety of people. Through conversation the design professional quickly grasps the inadequacy of stereotypes and begins to get a feel for the actual substance of another person's life. Though the plot and physical action of a disabled person's story may be very different from the designer's own, the emotions and responses will be readily understandable. A common result of a

designer's authentic effort to enter into a disabled person's experience and into the social and biographical contexts of disability is a heightened responsiveness to disability-related issues and, more important, a respect for the intent that
underlies accessibility codes, standards, and criteria.

Autobiographies and documentary films can also give architects a sense of the kinds of problems the environment poses
for disabled people. Though as "evidence" autobiography is by
definition anecdotal, the writer's feelings and observations can
convey to able-bodied designers an interpretation very different
from what they might expect. For example, in architectural par-
lance stairs function as a means of vertical circulation. Yet when
a wheelchair user writes about living upstairs (as Cheryl Davis
does in chapter 2), a complex and intriguing picture emerges.
The stairs are not merely physically difficult; they become the
stage for a human drama of family conflict and profound emotional discomfort. They are also a declaration: Disabled People
Excluded. An unsympathetic physical environment forces disabled people to endure such distress day after day. Through
autobiographical literature and biographical films, architects
can begin to understand the ways in which the existing physical
environment is a harsh and unforgiving place for millions of
people, one that both limits their lives and diminishes society's
perceptions of their abilities and personal worth.

Investigatory Methods

Architects can also turn to the social sciences, which have
developed several methods for gaining insight into the experiences of unfamiliar populations. Here let us briefly review three
such methods: simulation, unobtrusive observation, and ethnographic interviewing.

Simulation workshops in which able-bodied people temporarily "try on" a disability by using wheelchairs or blinders offer
participants some firsthand experience of the physical and
emotional aspects of disability.[5] But this tactic often backfires,

5. For an extremely sophisticated application of simulation techniques to
the perceptual problems of the elderly, see Leon Pastalan and D. H. Carson,

as it can generate so much anxiety that the participant over-
reacts, unable to understand or even believe that any but "su-
percrips" venture out alone or at all. For during a short-term
simulation a participant cannot develop adequate compensatory skills; nor does simulation enable participants to bear the
weight of cultural and social prejudices and expectations.

Unobtrusive observation has obvious benefits but two critical
drawbacks. First, although unobtrusive observers may feel they
are obtaining an "objective" view of a real-life situation—un-
tainted by the self-consciousness that those being observed
might feel if they knew they were being observed—unless the
observers already understand the issues they are likely to mis-
interpret what they are seeing. Second, unobtrusive observation, by definition, maintains a distance between observer and
observed; unless supplemented by other methods it does not
allow the able-bodied observer to cross the boundary between
self and other: The physical disabled people being observed
remain "them."

Ethnographic interviews that focus on the comparative analysis of able-bodied and disabled "cultures" can provide the interpretation of events that unobtrusive observation does not.
Interviews may be unstructured or may follow a predetermined
format.[6] Among the many topics worth pursuing, the following
questions will be of especial interest to architects:

What helps you orient yourself in a new place? (sounds, smells,
    wall signs, floor markings?)
What places outside your home do you regularly go to? (school,
    work, friends' houses, restaurants, movies, bank, post of-
    fice, grocery store, laundry?) How do you get there? Does
    the time of day or the weather affect your method of trans-
    portation or route? How often do you go out in the evening?

---

eds., *Spatial Behavior of Older People* (Ann Arbor: Institute of Gerontology, University of Michigan and Wayne State University, 1970).

6. For a more extensive discussion of ethnographic interviewing, and ex-
cerpts and summaries from interviews with physically disabled residents of
Berkeley, California, see Raymond Lifchez and Barbara Winslow, *Design for
Independent Living: The Environment and Physically Disabled People* (New York:
Whitney Library of Design, 1979; rpt. Berkeley and Los Angeles: University of
California Press, 1979).

How many people do you live with? Are any of them regularly involved in helping you with daily activities? Do you have an attendant? What sorts of activities do you need help with? What place in town would you most like to visit that you have not been able to visit? What prevents you from going there? What devices would you most like to see invented? (For the kitchen? bathroom? public transit? wheelchair attachment?) Do you feel stigmatized by separate entrances to public buildings?

A valuable variation on the ethnographic interview is what one might call a round-the-clock observation-interview. This technique involves spending extended periods of time (in six- to twenty-four-hour blocks) with an informant in order to observe and discuss all aspects of his or her daily life, from awakening to getting into bed.

New Models for User Participation

"User participation" has become a catchall term for a variety of efforts—both thoughtful and merely pro forma—to elicit the opinions of those who will actually live or work in a building or use its facilities. In its ideal form user participation allows knowledgeable representative users to participate actively and meaningfully in the planning and review of a new design. But, like any political process, user participation can be coopted or misapplied:

User participation will fail if the architect is not truly committed to consultation with laypersons in general or disabled laypersons in particular, or if the architect feels that user participation is but a time-consuming ritual that undermines professionalism or threatens the aesthetic integrity of the project.

For the well-intentioned architect, user participation will be meaningless if he or she does not know what questions to ask the users, how to interpret their answers, or how to apply their comments.

Even the well-intentioned and well-informed architect can hardly invite hundreds of users into the studio at each stage of review; nor will a randomly chosen sample of disabled laypersons necessarily understand what they are being shown.

As this chain of pitfalls suggests, user participation can be effective only if the architect has sufficient knowledge of the user groups to ask the right questions and derive useful generalizations from the users' answers and comments. In addition, the architect must develop a method for user participation that enables users to make relevant suggestions at the appropriate stage of the design process.

One method for "using the user" well is performance testing, a low-risk economical way to evaluate an existing site or explore the implications of a proposed design. This technique involves bringing representative users to a site in order to document (on paper or on videotape) how they negotiate the environment, what obstacles they encounter, and how they feel about being in that environment. Performance tests should be run at various times of day (and, for outdoor sites, under various weather conditions) to determine how nature's variations affect performance. The results of these observations and on-site interviews can be used to supplement any list of the site's deficiencies and hazards prepared from routine inspection. For example, to determine the number and location of proposed new emergency exits from an auditorium, one can place a variety of people around the auditorium and stage a fire alarm. Measurements of how long it takes each individual to locate and reach the emergency exits and their reports of the obstacles they encountered will provide invaluable information.

Video or eight-millimeter film documentation of performance tests allows designers both to study particular scenes and to share portions of the footage with other designers, other users, and clients. The camera should be positioned to approximate the user's field of vision; it may be mounted on the back of a wheelchair or held at the proper height by an accompanying party. A wide-angle lens with preset aperture and focus can be adjusted to record one frame every half second. The footage will be somewhat choppy and flat, but the simplicity of operation allows the photographer to capture a reasonably accurate view without repeatedly adjusting the equipment. Still photographs supplemented by an audiotape can also provide striking visual documentation.[7]

The single most useful method for working with informants is what we call the interview-in-place. Here the informant is asked to select a place (a room at home, a cafe, his or her workplace) in which he or she feels comfortable speaking about that place as a physical and social setting. The setting itself will generate a variety of topics for discussion: What physical and social factors make the setting noteworthy for the informant? How does he or she feel being in that setting and going to and from it? Of course, more personal comments will arise in more personal settings, in the informant's bedroom or kitchen, for example.[8]

Compliance versus Commitment

Access is not just another constraint on architectural design; it is a major perceptual orientation to humanity. In order to achieve it, architects must confront a range of human issues for which there are no simple technical solutions. And since only very few practicing architects have those disabilities that most challenge traditional ideas about design, guidance will not come from inside the profession. Architects must actively seek out disabled people to assist them. The first step in this process is for the architect to become fully self-aware, so as not to inadvertently stigmatize clients who are disabled, or elderly, or very young.

Renovating society's house, which is one way to perceive the built environment, is a profound work. To restructure the environment so that it responds better to the needs of all requires that a significant number of people—not only architects

7. For a discussion of video documentation, see Lifchez and Winslow, *Design for Independent Living*, 138–42.

8. Interview-in-place was the primary method used in the extensive interviews presented in Lifchez and Winslow, *Design for Independent Living*, which contains a description of the process (pp. 135–37) and extensive reports of such interviews.

but clients and managers and all others who are concerned with the built environment—reevaluate their thinking. All must come to believe that an environment that is more responsive to the needs of "real people" is not only possible but desirable. Designers operate within a political context, and in order to implement real change they must be more sensitive and forward thinking than others. The architect must be prepared to point out to clients in the public and private sectors that the new standards and code provisions for accessibility should not be perceived as unusual or burdensome but rather as the latest requirement placed by consensus on the environment. The architect as visionary must remind others that architecture reflects how society feels about itself, that creating an environment is a dynamic process, and that architecture should express a society's highest aspirations and ideals.

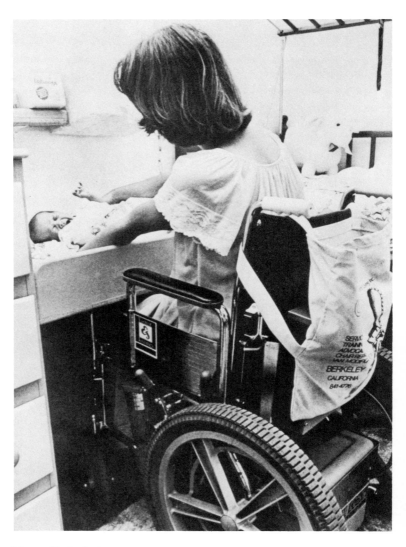

Many able-bodied people falsely assume that disabled people are entirely a group apart or that they differ from able-bodied people only in their dimensional requirements. But architects and designers must make more subtle differentiations, to consider their clients' social and emotional needs, and to be especially attentive to the ways the differences and similarities between the able-bodied and the disabled overlap. (Photo by Jane Scherr; from Raymond Lifchez and Barbara Winslow, *Design for Independent Living* [California, 1981])

4

Clients as People

Raymond Lifchez

Architectural Design with the Physically Disabled User in Mind was originally conceived as a year-long multicampus experiment. Each school was to offer a studio course that would allow students to work day-to-day with several physically disabled design consultants. The actual curriculum and the nature of the design problems to be assigned were left to the discretion of the chief instructor at each school. This chapter presents an overview of the pedagogy and curriculum at U. C. Berkeley.

I had conceived of Architectural Design with the Physically Disabled User in Mind as a pedagogical experiment with several interlocking objectives. Principally, I hoped that we could develop a method for placing client accommodation at the heart of the studio curriculum. Although the suitability of a design is always judged against the perspective of the client—his or her needs, values, and expectations—this theme is the least articulated, least developed as a teachable subject. While certain standards have emerged among architectural schools about undergraduate instruction in design, there is no consensus about how to introduce the client's perspective in the teaching of the design process.

To achieve this principal objective, I envisioned a studio course that would offer students repeated opportunities to carefully examine their own values, attitudes, and expectations and also to begin to relate more empathetically to a universe of prospective clients. We wanted our students thus to better articulate their own values and to become more aware of how those values serve as a filter through which as professionals they would perceive their clients and interpret their clients' needs. At the same time, we wanted our students to begin to think about clients from the inside, as idiosyncratic individuals, rather than merely as abstract user groups with quantifiable functional requirements. From the daily interactions with our physically disabled design consultants we hoped our students would acquire a sense of the variety and complexity of human needs, preferences, assumptions, emotions, and expectations. Through the twin processes of looking inward and looking outward, self-examination and empathic imagination, we hoped to instil in our students both a sense of personal and professional humility and a vital curiosity about the clients who would be their partners in shaping the built environment.

Within this context of client accommodation, we wanted our students to come to perceive the special needs of physically disabled people as a particularly pointed and complex instance of a universal concept: Every client has some special needs and preferences, which the good architect will discover and work from. In this way we felt we could achieve our second principal objective: to place the environmental and psychosocial needs of physically disabled people into the mainstream of the architectural curriculum. For although our design consultants were physically disabled, our course was not intended to isolate the problems of the physically disabled but rather to integrate those problems into the general set of problems every architect faces.

At the beginning of the course, we expected that most of our students would have a rather one-dimensional understanding of people different from themselves, that our students would tend to view people in large, undifferentiated classes defined by one or two overarching characteristics. For example, we assumed that most students would see elderly people as a homogeneous group whose lives are rather uniformly determined by their age; similarly, we guessed that our students would view physically disabled people solely as an occasion to discuss technical problems of physical mobility. During the semester we hoped that our students would come to gain a broader sense of the ways in which labels like "elderly" and "disabled" artificially cluster hundreds of thousands of individuals, each of whom has a unique set of qualities and needs—physical and medical, intellectual and psychosocial, vocational and recreational, and so on—and each of whom has an emotional and psychological interior life.

These objectives and expectations served as the scaffolding for our studio course. But, like architects in the studio, educators in the classroom, or scientists in the lab—for we were all three—we wanted also to maintain a sense of purposeful vagueness in our investigations. That is, we did not want to reduce our objectives to a set of directives, but rather to keep our process open enough to allow both instructors and students to be surprised by the unexpected, enlightened by the unpredictable.

Design Problems

Like any studio course, our class was based on a set of design problems, but our procedures differed from the traditional format in three essential ways: the writing of hypothetical client biographies, the active participation of physically disabled design consultants, and the establishment of design teams. I will explain these procedures and their rationale in the course of describing the kinds of design problems we assigned to our students.

On the first day of class we assigned an architectural sketch problem, giving students a week to complete it. Students were accustomed to doing sketch problems, and to begin the course with one, plunging directly into the subject of architectural design, seemed to appeal to them. This assignment was intended to acquaint students with the social and architectural issues the course would address and to enable us to evaluate their graphic skills in presenting architectural ideas. We also used these initial sketches as a projective measure of the students' attitudes on entering the course.

The format of the sketch problem was to renovate an existing space for a new use: for example, to convert an old house into a small cafe, a grocery into a health club, a bank into a twenty-four-hour variety store, or a garage into a community center. No instructions were given regarding access requirements, although the design consultants were in the studio when the sketch problem was explained, and we mentioned that they would be available for consultation throughout the week. In addition to the usual requirements of presenting a design that realized their interpretation of the new program, students were to write short biographical sketches of the users they had in mind as they conceived the design.

The completed sketch problems were reviewed by the instructors, design consultants, and students. The discussion first turned to the appropriate use of space, circulation, style, and similar basic themes. From there we were able to raise questions about the assumptions the designers had made concerning the users, noting especially any stereotyping in their characterizations of users. Students seemed to take these discussions openmindedly—and expressed a certain surprise at the attitudes their sketches revealed. Many students said that while working on the problem they had felt a conflict between what they themselves genuinely enjoy about personal interactions in public spaces and what they had believed their task to be as architects proposing a design.

We then assigned the design problem that the students, working in self-selected design teams of six to eight members, would address for the remainder of the term. The design teams were to assume that a neighborhood group of small private investors had commissioned them to design a one-square-block facility that would allow for residential, commercial, and recreational uses. All the teams were assigned the same real site in a nearby, demographically heterogeneous neighborhood. They were expected to familiarize themselves with the neighborhood and its diverse ethnic enclaves, age cohorts, and income groups so that they could write and refine a set of credible biographies for their hypothetical clients. As the designs evolved, they were to write scenarios that showed the clients in their new environment.

At the end of the term each team was to present an eighth-inch (1:96) three-dimensional model of its design, complete with appropriately scaled furniture and photographs of representative clients acting out the scenarios. The construction posed an enjoyable challenge to our students' inventiveness, and their ingenious methods and materials made the studio an exciting place to be. The final models were large enough and flexible enough for our "lay" design consultants to interpret accurately the spaces represented and thus to participate actively in the critiques. Students were also prompted to rig up mirrors to enable wheelchair users to see into the models, and to devise tactile cues to aid our blind consultants in their critiques.

A handful of other premises and rules governed these design problems. In terms of construction, students were limited to simple domestic materials (wood, simple masonry) and had to respect a three-story height limit. Their buildings were expected to comply with all relevant legal requirements for residential and commercial construction, and we specified for them the number of people who would occupy the site. The distribution of space among the various purposes and users, however, was left to the students. We also told the class to assume that their clients could afford to live in the new facility—a not wholly realistic, but pedagogically useful, assumption that relieved them from analyses of economics and enabled them to focus on architectural and social factors.

The form and premises of this design problem reflected several pedagogical considerations. We wanted to pose a design problem whose physical scale was commensurate with our students' abilities but whose functional requirements were complex. We chose real sites in local neighborhoods so that students and design consultants could develop a common frame of reference from firsthand explorations of the site. Each term we selected for our students a heterogeneous urban neighborhood, usually one that was undergoing demographic and economic transition, as a way of introducing students to the difficulties of interpreting a complex setting.

Our requirement that students work in self-selected design teams reflected two pedagogical intentions. First, we thought teamwork would shift the primary emphasis from student-instructor relations to student-to-student discourse. Rather than acquiescing to the instructors' authority or trying to second-guess the instructors' preferences, the students had to work together to convince one another about how to proceed. Second, we hoped teamwork would both strengthen and healthily undermine the rational component of our students' problem-solving skills. Their analytic skills would be sharpened as they had to explain and defend their assumptions and choices to teammates, as teams discussed, argued, synthesized, refined, or rejected individual members' proposals. But the inherent "messiness" of teamwork also required students to cope with the nonrational and irrational, with one another's emotional and intuitive energies, defenses and attitudes.

As I noted earlier, the students' designs had to meet legal standards for new construction, but we did not instruct them to exceed those requirements as regards access for physically disabled people. For example, we did not demand that every residential unit be fully accessible. We gave our students information about the mechanics of access, and the instructors and design consultants were always on hand to answer technical questions. But each team had to decide who would be using their facility and how much emphasis to place on accessibility. For example, students had to ask themselves how many residential units they thought should be accessible and whether ramps or elevators were the better solution for particular entryways. Did they want to cluster the apartments for the disabled and elderly on the ground floor (in order to simplify access to these units from the street) or did they want to avoid creating a "ghetto" by distributing such units throughout their facility?

As the course progressed, the students' questions regarding access became more specific and sensitive:

Should we implement a solution that enhances access for someone with one kind of disability but denies access for those with some other disability?

Should an architecturally elegant solution—a spiral staircase, sleeping loft, sunken bathtub—that appeals to able-bodied clients be abandoned because it cannot be used by physically disabled clients?

If an able-bodied couple has a physically disabled friend, will that friend be offended if he cannot visit their apartment or can visit only in the kitchen but not gain access to the living room?

Our approach to these and similar questions was always to encourage our students to make well-reasoned choices that they each could feel good about and, at the same time, to acknowledge openly the social and aesthetic implications of their choices and tradeoffs. We urged them to take the course of action they felt most comfortable with and to execute it as well as possible. As a solution was developed its inherent worth became more apparent, as did its inherent weaknesses as an architectural design and as a social statement.

Because each class consisted of between sixty and eighty students, the architectural designs represented a large range of solutions (and attitudes) that were usefully compared during in-class critiques. The subject of access was never reduced to easy mechanistic solutions. Its enormous complexity as a social issue was always before us but always as only one of many social considerations.

Evaluative Measures

Since our courses were part of a curricular experiment, we devised a set of evaluative measures that would enable us to gauge our success in meeting our objectives. Of course, as instructors we evaluated our students' performance on the design problems, and, as might be expected, their designs provided us with the best insight into how their thinking changed over the term. We also monitored students' responses to critiques and daily consultations with instructors and design consultants, and their responses to readings, lectures, and occasional films.

These evaluations were supplemented by various kinds of direct and indirect assessments; indeed, part of our experiment was to discover which types of assessments yielded useful information about students' development. In any given term we used several, but not all, of the following measures:

Indirect Assessments
> Prequestionnaire to assess attitudes and knowledge at the beginning of the term
> Postquestionnaire to assess attitudes and knowledge at the end of the term
> Semantic differential

Direct Assessments
> Reading students' journals
> In-depth interviews (conducted by the outside observers)
> Site observations (made by the outside observers)

Let me briefly describe each of these measures.

Sociometric questionnaires. The pre- and postquestionnaires contained items about students' experience with physically disabled people and their attitudes toward them. We had originally hoped to administer the pre- and postquestionnaire each term, but when students complained of "psychological overload" we dropped the second measure. We were, however, able to draw three inferences from comparing the prequestionnaires and the students' performance in the course:

Students who had befriended, worked with, or otherwise been engaged with physically disabled people did the best work in the studio.

Students with no such personal experience leaned toward stereotyped images of disability and tended to work less with the consultants.

Students who had a family member or very close friend who

was physically disabled were the most knowledgeable about the subject of disability but also the most ambivalent about working with the consultants and somewhat less imaginative in their architectural solutions to access problems.

Semantic differential. At the request of the Exxon Education Foundation that we include at least one quantitative measure, we asked Dr. Nancy Crewe, a psychologist at the University of Minnesota Medical School, to prepare a semantic differential measure.[1] This measure was intended to assess students' attitudes toward two key concepts (accessible design and the use of design teams) and two client groups (physically disabled people and elderly people). Although the data derived from the semantic differential confirmed that students' attitudes toward the key concepts and two client groups changed in the hoped-for direction, students disliked the measure, complaining that it smacked of mysterious psychological manipulation. For this reason, we used the semantic differential during only four of the six terms we taught the course.

Journals. During the fourth term of the project Wendy Sarkissian, a visiting scholar who served as our site observer, recommended that we ask students to keep journals. We decided to offer students the option of receiving additional course units for keeping a daily journal. Those who elected this option were expected to make their entries outside of class and to record the time, place, and mood for each entry. In turn, we read their journals at three scheduled dates during the term and responded with lengthy written comments about the journal's contents, the student's performance in the studio, and the relationship between the two. We also promised that we would keep confidential what we read.

Between one-fifth and one-half of the students elected to write a journal. The interchange of written commentary pro-

1. The semantic differential presents respondents with a set of bipolar adjectives (good-bad, strong-weak, active-passive) and asks them to rate a set of variables (e.g., 1 = bad, 7 = good). For a complete discussion of the technique by its creators, see C. E. Osgood, G. J. Suci, and P. H. Tannenbaum, *The Measurement of Meaning* (Urbana: University of Illinois Press, 1961).

duced pleasant and constructive feelings between journal-keepers and journal-readers, and students often came to office hours to discuss our comments on their entries. As instructors, we felt that this additional contact and rapport aided students in their studio work. As evaluators, we discovered that some of the most thoughtful, personal, and imaginative commentaries about the project came from these journals.

Interviews and on-site observations. Each term we contracted a social scientist unaffiliated with the school of architecture to serve as our outside observer. These observers had all previously worked professionally with physically disabled people, and some had also worked with architects. We asked them to serve as both evaluators and facilitators. As evaluators, they were to sit in on studio sessions to observe the interactions between instructors, design consultants, and students and also to interview a sampling of these three groups. The students were told that all interview material would be kept confidential and that the instructors would not even know who had been interviewed, much less what was said, until the entire project had ended. Indeed, we asked the observers not to tell us anything about their in-class observations unless they felt that without their intervention we were in danger of imperiling the entire project. (As it turned out, such intervention proved necessary in the first term of the project; see chapter 5.)

We also asked the observers to serve as facilitators—in effect, as listening posts: nonpartisan, nonjudgmental confidants to whom students, design consultants, and instructors could unburden themselves of their anxieties, uncertainties, and resentments. We knew that our course would place unusual emotional demands on all participants, and we hoped that the presence of a skilled neutral party would help relieve the inevitable stress and tensions.

Report Cards

In the following eight chapters readers will hear from instructors, design consultants, students, and outside observers who participated in the project. But here I want to comment generally on several central issues.

At Berkeley the project ran for six terms, during which some three hundred students were enrolled. For almost all our students, the presence of the design consultants in the studio made a profound impression. At the beginning of each term, many students were noticeably fearful; some seemed excited by the new challenge, some ashamed of a voyeuristic curiosity. We witnessed throughout the term a variety of defensive strategies: Some students largely ignored the design consultants and silently skirted the issue of access; some openly complained that they resented the intrusion of "sociology" into the studio; yet others scurried to satisfy the consultants' every suggestion, without independently weighing the merit of their advice.

But the vast majority of students who applied themselves conscientiously and honestly did well: Their architectural skills improved markedly during the term, and their final designs showed an imaginative and practical integration of people and environment. Overall the biggest challenge was posed by the difficulties of working in a group. Some of the design teams proved unable to discover for themselves an effective method for working together, and their designs reflected the failure of their group process, showing little human interaction and providing few areas for such interaction. Several groups devised insincere machinations to disguise unresolved conflicts. One student, for example, admitted, "We felt we should have a communal kitchen as a symbol of togetherness, even if no one believes anyone would really use it. Besides, the instructors like communal arrangements."

Our end-of-term surveys and interviews revealed that most of our students took the course to heart. The attitudinal measures showed positive changes in the students' feelings about and perceptions of physically disabled people. But, as might be expected, the students' final designs were more instructive than the survey data. The way in which a design team organized and apportioned space, for example, reflected team members' values (toward ecological issues, the nuclear family, private property, urban aesthetics) and also their group psyche. Cohesive and confident teams tended to design open accessible plans that invited interaction with adjacent properties, while less confident teams opted for more closed plans that were more isolated from the rest of the neighborhood.

The final models also reflected a variety of biases and uncertainties. Students seemed unable, for example, to imagine what elderly people do other than lose themselves in nostalgia, watch neighborhood children play, and keep house. Although many of the designs featured communal recreation and gathering places for young and able-bodied residents, few elderly or physically disabled residents were featured in these scenarios. These residents were never shown to use communal areas such as saunas, hot tubs, or sun-bathing decks—areas where partial or total nudity is acceptable.

Students also assumed that mobility was the fundamental problem facing physically disabled individuals. Although we had hoped that students would acquire through conversations with the design consultants some sense of the multiple physiological problems that accompany disability, it seems that students were too reserved to ask questions that might be perceived as too personal. As a result, their designs for paraplegics and quadriplegics made no provisions for the indispensable attendants. And students incorrectly assumed that wheelchair users could simply be hauled from one spot to another without physical hazard or inconvenience.

We also observed that those design teams that created a family with a physically disabled child usually placed the family in some remote corner of the building. Students explained that they assumed that having a disabled child causes such stress in the family that the parents would prefer more privacy than other residents; the students' underlying rationale, however, seems to have been that parents would want to hide their child, using the environment to mask their differences from other families.

Such observations of students' designs and their relation to the outcomes of our evaluative measures became a valuable part of the instructors' collaborative efforts. These materials were, after all, a projection of how we had taught, of what we intended to say and what our students heard us say, of how we hoped our students would feel about their work with physically disabled people, and of how we individually felt about the relevance of our course to the practice of architecture.

All the instructors had enthusiastically joined the experiment, approving of the approach to the course and the material to be used. Yet during the first weeks, confronted for the first time by physically disabled people in an architectural design studio, some instructors found themselves uncomfortable or inconvenienced by having to teach in a way that was meaningful to the students and also to the design consultants, who themselves were attempting simultaneously to learn about the course and to serve as consultants. I recall an early staff meeting when we discussed the problem posed by three-way conversations between instructor, student, and design consultant. We were afraid that students would ignore the consultants altogether, listening and responding only to the instructor. One instructor observed that several instructors tended to exclude the design consultants from the conversation, perhaps listening but not responding to what they said, or even positioning themselves to sit or stand in between the students and consultants. Several instructors then complained that they had not been prepared for this aspect of the work and that including the design consultants seemed to take more time than it was worth given the number of students in the studio.

Such discussions occurred at several staff meetings, each time with slight variations and new nuances. To some extent the observers were able to ameliorate the situation, but frequently even their interventions were felt to be an intrusion by persons who were neither architects nor academic staff.

At the end of each term these materials became a touchstone by which we, the instructors, were able to review our own process constructively and in some detail. As the third term began, we had become rather adept at handling the course and ourselves. And in each successive term, we and the course improved measurably, as the students' designs indicated.

Students were asked to create two-dimensional collages as a first step in mapping the scenarios for their imaginary clients. The collages expose crucial issues of values, preferences, and feelings about the environment's uses, physical properties (light, heat, sound), and subjective qualities (intimacy, hospitality). The ensuing classroom discussions alert the students to the range of issues they will need to examine in order to understand their clients—and themselves—as they search for design solutions.

5

Hidden Agendas

Raymond Lifchez

The Architectural Design with the Physically Disabled User in Mind project was based on the assumption that architecture students would have internalized our culture's negative attitudes toward physically disabled people, and our major task, as we perceived it, would be to deal with these biases as they became manifest in the studio. But we were soon made painfully aware by the outside observers, who were monitoring the work day-to-day, that first the instructors needed to confront their own fears and attitudes about disability and disabled people. Our goodwill and intelligence did not prevent us from having subconscious expectations or assumptions, nor did our stated agreement on the course's goals preclude our having tacit personal agendas.

The original proposal for the Architectural Design with the Physically Disabled User in Mind project called for five schools to develop undergraduate studio courses that would fulfill the objectives of the traditional studio course and address three additional objectives: to sensitize students to the architectural implications and environmental requirements of a disabled population; to integrate the active participation of disabled consumers, represented by the design consultants, into the design process; and to demonstrate that inclusiveness and exemplary design are compatible.

During the planning stages we expected that in implementing these articulated goals individual instructors would, of course, introduce a secondary set of objectives that represented their personal approach to design and education. For example, I knew that my curriculum would emphasize a group approach to design, involve the creation of client biographies and scenarios, and entail the construction of large-scale three-dimensional models to be peopled by scale photographs of clients.

We also expected that each instructor, consultant, and student would have a private agenda. Students, for example, might want to meet new classmates, become more adept at photography and model construction, learn more about disability, and—yes—improve their grade-point averages.

In particular, we knew from the start that the consultants' presence would bring about changes in the ways we taught and students learned. Our theme was to be accommodation. We knew we had to fully integrate our consultants into the course, lest they become mere ornaments or spokesmen for those in whom we avowed a sincere interest. We sought to actively assimilate our consultants into the design process, not simply to leave it up to them to find their own way.

In order to achieve this accommodation, we knew we had three problems to overcome:

We did not want our course to be seen by others as a special course in barrier-free architectural design. Such a perception would hinder our effectiveness in teaching students that access for physically disabled people is fundamental, not incidental, to the design of a building, whatever its purpose.

We wanted the consultants to feel that both staff and students viewed their role in the studio as a valid and valuable one. We hoped the consultants would eventually see tangible evidence of their effort imprinted on students' designs.

We wanted our students to relate to the design consultants as consultants and not as clients. That is, we wanted them to consider what the consultants said, to evaluate it, and to accept or reject advice according to their own understanding of what the design exercises asked of them as architects. We did not want students simply to acquiesce to the consultants—to take orders or slavishly incorporate every suggestion, every personal need into their designs. Nor did we want students to sidestep any discomfort in confronting the consultants' disabilities simply by trying to please. The consultations were to impel the students to take account of a range of complex human issues, not merely to settle for a set of architectural solutions.

In addition, the inauguration of the project effected two other significant changes in the course as I had previously taught it. The course was to be monitored by outside observers, whose charge was to gather data about all aspects of the project and present an analysis that would supplement the project's final report, which was to be prepared by the instructors and consultants. (The outside observers were not to reveal or discuss any of their findings until after the completion of the entire project, unless at a given point they felt that such discussion was crucial to the project's continuing.) We now also had the resources to administer a variety of pre- and post-test measures that would allow us to see whether our efforts produced any significant changes in our students' attitudes and feelings. These evaluative data would supplement the perceptions we would gain from critiques of the students' designs.

All these issues were foreseen by the staff when we began. Some of us had worked together before, other staff members were new. At the time none of us realized how difficult it would be to organize our various "constituencies"—instructors, consultants, student design teams, outside observers—into a coherent working group. Nor did we realize how deeply affected we each were by the negative stance the profession and the schools had taken regarding the recently enacted federal laws that mandated full civil rights for the disabled. In essence, the legally imposed access requirement caused architects to confront a new and powerful concept: that the needs of people who had heretofore been unconsciously viewed as less than fully human and less than deserving would now begin to reshape the environment for the rest of us. We were just beginning to understand the social and political context in which the subject of access is embedded.

Stage Fright

As the first semester of the project began, I was beset by a roomful of fears. The hoopla that had accompanied the securing of the Exxon grant was unsettling: Could I live up to everyone's expectations? Were the tasks we were about to propose to our students beyond them at this stage of their development? How would the outside observers' monitoring affect the students' performance? How well prepared were we to validate the presence of the design consultants, few of whom had worked with architecture students before and whose physical disabilities included blindness, deafness, mobility impairments, and speech impairments? I felt particularly vulnerable because I was coming up for tenure that year. And now four instructors, six design consultants, three outside architectural consultants, and three outside research observers awaited my first move.

During the first weeks of the first course we made a lot of mistakes, as these comments by Michael Rolfson, a social psychologist serving as an outside observer, illustrate:

The design consultants' input into the review seemed to be largely ignored by the students. The general pattern for involving the design consultants in the critique was to wait until a natural pause in the flow (after thirty to forty-five minutes) and then ask if they had any comments. The consultants' participation seemed to be an afterthought, not an integral part of the review. The response to design consultants' remarks took one of two forms: either the instructor commented briefly before going on to something else, or the remark was not responded to at all. There was virtually no direct communication between students and design consultants—any communication was mediated by an instructor. The physical arrangement of students, instructors, and consultants around the model under review generally had the model between the reviewer and the design consultants. The focus of attention of the students was thus directed almost exclusively away from the design consultants. The posture of the students when standing close to a consultant resembled that of people forced to be close together, like riding in an elevator. Whenever possible students chose to arrange themselves by placing distance between themselves and the consultants.

There was a barrier between the design consultants and the students and all of the teaching staff, with the exception of Lifchez, which resulted in covert exclusion of the consultants. Disability seemed to be the barrier. Students seemed to respond with a degree of suspicion toward me as well as toward the design consultants, since they had not been told exactly what we were there for. Lifchez, in his anxiety that the theme of disability would stigmatize this course and thus jeopardize the validity of the subject he hoped to establish in the standard curriculum, had not told students much about the project or the intended role of the design consultants.

Through a series of meetings led by Rolfson, we were able to begin to unsnarl the situation. The most important activities at this point were to inform the students about the project and the roles of the design consultants and outside observers, to improve communication between the instructors and the consultants, to help the instructors serve as role models for the students in relating to the consultants, and to clarify our individual tasks and responsibilities.

By the end of the first course we had made substantial progress. Again, Rolfson came to observe:

The process of interaction among the participants at the final critique of student work reflected a major shift from the previous reviews. The design consultants were included structurally, verbally, and nonverbally by students and in general by the teaching staff. The level of trust was sufficiently high that students not only communicated directly with the consultants but also constructively disagreed with them at times. There seemed to be no confusion among the students about the role the consultants were to play in the critiques. The level of comfort around sensitive social issues was, with one exception, quite high.

At this time, the end of winter quarter of 1979, we invited to Berkeley representatives of the four other schools who would be giving similar courses in the spring. We purposefully placed the emphasis on the problems we had encountered: the role unconscious assumptions and covert politics had played in shaping our process. After several days of talk, we parted in great spirits.

But the interim reports we later received from each school as it began its new semester were depressing, as were the reports of the roving project monitor (a sociologist) who visited each school in turn to observe and to interview a sample of participants (students, consultants, and administrators).

At one school the instructor quickly discovered that the studio space assigned to his class was up a flight of stairs: inaccessible! He was reluctant to ask for another studio: He knew that his colleagues had reservations about the direction his teaching was taking and he did not want to call attention to himself. He had also, some months before, decided to pursue a tentative job offer at another university and knew he would need the support of his present colleagues to obtain the new job. Trapped by covert politics, he remained in the inaccessible studio. His students worked exclusively with two blind consultants, whose participation was useful but was not balanced by sighted individuals with other kinds of disabilities.

At another school, a well-known expert on the subject of access had decided to take on the project personally, assisted by a group of other instructors. The particular studio course chosen for the project was one in which juniors with one year of professional work experience (a work-study program) were to be judged as to their preparedness for the final year of the program, the thesis year. The students had known that the course would be demanding, but they felt trapped and angry when they learned that it was to focus on the subject of access, with which they had no experience, and that their principal instructor was to be an acknowledged expert on the subject.

Department politics here too took their toll: The principal instructor had encountered opposition from his faculty when he had earlier tried to "modernize" the school's curriculum. As faculty opposition to his proposal increased, he responded by being out of town on school business as often as possible—despite his commitment to lead the studio course. Our roving site observer noted that even after the term was well underway, the studio space was cluttered and no attempt was made to make it accessible to a consultant who used a wheelchair: a certain, if perhaps unconscious, expression of the students' and instructors' hostility toward the project. Certainly the subject of accessibility would have personal associations for those students in their professional careers, but not the associations we had hoped to establish.

At another school, the covert politics were more bizarre still. The professor chosen to run the project was a visiting European architect with a reputation abroad for his work in retrofitting buildings for access. He was eager to become a tenured professor at an American university, and his American colleagues hoped that his reputation would secure for the school's faculty some lucrative contracts. Working for his department chairman's private firm helped to entrench him in the school. As it happened, one of the private firm's clients, the director of a medical center, took a strong interest in our project and arranged to have several of his center's physically disabled staff members volunteer to serve as design consultants in the studio course. This arrangement delighted the professor and his department head, as perhaps they envisioned a contract for the design of new medical center facilities.

During the course of the project, it seems, this professor seized every opportunity to exhibit his ability; his presence, his ideas, his reputation commanded the scene, leaving little room for others to affect the course of the project. The designs developed by his students were highly dramatic, futuristic solutions that bore little relationship to their stated purposes.

At the last school, unrelated circumstances again shaped the project for the students. The professor, one of the most popular in the department, had never had difficulty in attracting good students to his design courses. Unfortunately, the course he was to teach was for second-semester seniors, and he felt that to keep them interested as graduation approached he had to give them something exotic, a final project that would indulge their imaginations. So he chose a design problem he thought would be irresistible: a famous waterfront urban renewal property in a glamorous city thousands of miles away from the campus. To warm students up to the project, he had the local rehabilitation center put everyone through a serious empathic simulation, with wheelchairs, disabling devices, and such.

The fatal flaw in his plan was that neither the students nor the design consultants had ever been to the distant city in question. For them the site seemed but a vague place. The color slides certainly did not elucidate the mystery city for the course's blind design consultant. The professor's heartfelt effort to keep his students excited during their last bout with school had lured him into selecting a design project completely inappropriate for our purposes. Even for sighted participants, slides were insufficient to establish a common ground for discussion about how people relate to the built environment.

In sum, although each school's project director had agreed to our set of project goals, the courses were vastly different, with the greatest variation pertaining to the very core of the project: sensitizing students to the needs of disabled users and integrating active user participation into the design process. At one school the introduction of the design consultants into the studio was viewed largely as a tactic to shock students into a recognition of disabled users' needs; at another, the consultants were treated as resource persons, not active participants.

Of course, we had fully expected the classes to differ. But we had hoped that the multicampus experiment would demonstrate that our methods could be successfully adapted to each school's particular pedagogical philosophy and curriculum. We had known all along that any curriculum innovation would inevitably produce some degree of intradepartmental squabbling and student perturbance, and we never assumed that every instructor, consultant, and student would saintfully sacrifice his or her personal agenda for the good of the project.

But we had thought that the core objectives of the project could be faithfully fulfilled.

I felt disappointed by the results at the four sites. But my experiences at Berkeley had convinced me that we had "something" valuable to impart—something that went beyond issues of curriculum to issues of values, intentions, and use of authority. Our process was not yet ready for wholesale export to other campuses. I had also come to realize how much attention, time, and effort the project at Berkeley entailed. Thus we decided to discontinue the project at the four other schools and concentrate our efforts and resources at Berkeley.

Students as Research Subjects

As we continued at Berkeley, a great deal of progress on the research aspects of the project was made quarter by quarter. At the end of each course the students' work, performance, and attitudes toward the class were in many ways increasingly positive. Judging by their work—their final designs and oral presentations—and their comments on the department's official evaluation forms, which are submitted without signatures, we were largely succeeding in our pedagogical objectives.

But the monitoring process, which had to be attended to almost daily, was problematic. It made the course different from the school's other studio courses and made some students express doubts (which others probably silently shared) about our "real" objectives in teaching this course: Were they our students or our research subjects? Other students felt that the research aspect of the course added a certain importance to it: that the analyses of what they were doing would be used to help others. They seemed to enjoy the numerous visitors who regularly came to take a look. And the ongoing presence of a half-dozen physically disabled design consultants moving freely among the drafting tables and architectural models in motorized wheelchairs or with guide dogs added another measure of publicness and liveliness to the setting.

From time to time, then, we worried that we had unwittingly allowed another conflict into the agenda. The close attention paid to every aspect of a student's performance was a double-edged sword. It made each student more self-aware but also more self-conscious, more observant and self-critical but also more vulnerable. There was a real discomfort in being watched, but the process taught them how to watch. For many it was a wrenching experience: being confronted as never before, certainly not in a classroom, by the unfamiliar in themselves and in the world. In meeting these unexpected challenges with resources they never knew they had, our students experienced the disquieting aches and hard-earned satisfactions of personal and professional growth.

But I am not of the mind that teaches swimming by throwing initiates in over their heads, with words of commanding encouragement. Although the monitoring and testing added energy and purpose to our agenda, we had to ask whether we could have achieved as much with less tension and anxiety.

The simple answer is yes and no. Following Rolfson's recommendations, we made ongoing efforts each term to clarify for our students the nature of the research component of the project. After the first quarter of the project, we introduced the observers and researchers to the students at the very beginning of each term. As we explained their roles, we were sure to mention that they would not in any way be involved in grading the students' work. From end-of-term questionnaires and interviews with students, we continued to develop and refine guidelines for the research. In response to student complaints, we agreed to administer the researchers' pre- and post-tests only on days when no studio assignment was due. We also took more time to explain that these pre- and post-tests were tools to evaluate the course and to sample students' opinions, not to judge individual character, performance, or knowledge.

We tried to address students' concerns at being "guinea pigs," indeed to encourage them to express those concerns; we were wary of misinterpreting their silent compliance as acceptance or approval of the process. Some tensions proved intractable. Despite our explanations, there were always students who suspected that hidden purposes were involved, that the pre- and post-tests would reveal things about them that others had no right to know, that they were being judged in ways they neither fully understood nor condoned.

Of course, we never perfected our research process. Still, I remain convinced that the classroom, especially large classes that are offered regularly, is fertile territory in which to do hard research. In the social sciences, for example, it is not unusual for an instructor who teaches a large undergraduate lecture course to use the opportunity, and the students, in a research project, one usually unrelated to the course material. Many professors have partly built their careers on such research. The students represent a selected population whose responses can be correlated with statistical certainty. Whether or not they like being subjects, they have little recourse but to go along. Any psychic discomfort students might experience can be justified as a trade-off for giving them experiential knowledge of the scientific method in the profession they aspire to join. These students' main complaint seems to be never learning what was discovered. The results are slow to materialize and their publication, usually in professional journals, is even slower.

However, when the subject of the course is architecture rather than psychology, professors' and students' assumptions about research in the classroom are different. Students are not prepared for it, especially when more is involved than simple pre- and post-test questionnaires (How did you like this class? Did it meet your expectations?). We were asking our students to be subjects for eleven weeks, and we wanted to prepare them for this role without making them unnecessarily self-conscious, without spoiling their naturalness and open-mindedness.

In the architecture studio there is another, even more significant and elusive issue to confront. Architecture faculty and students seem to share a deep and largely unconscious belief that talent for architecture is a natural gift that could be damaged if scrutinized. This is an old belief, which places a certain edge on the kind of work we do, and I was well aware of it at the outset. Insofar as I was able, I made an effort to impress on our staff the importance of creating a "good climate" in which students would feel that they were in good hands. We all agreed that the means by which we would achieve our goals were no less important than those goals, and that our students' emotional and intellectual awakening required a truly humane and supportive classroom environment.

The day-to-day interactions in the studio and the designs our students produced reinforced our elementary but profound assumption: The *way* architecture students are taught about others greatly affects their understanding of what is presented in the studio and their eventual application of lessons learned to their professional lives. There is no substitute for face-to-face contact in acquiring the necessary knowledge of other people's needs, desires, and abilities; physical disability and architectural access are heartless abstractions unless taught within the context of human experience.

Observing and evaluating ourselves, being observed and evaluated by others, we came to be quite competent at this approach to teaching architectural design. I urge others to try it. The educational benefits—to both students and instructors—are immense.

"Yuji's mirror" is an example of how students tried to accommodate the physical needs of the design consultants. When held at various angles, the mirror enabled consultants who used wheelchairs to see the upper levels and interiors of the models.

6

Using the User Well

Cheryl Davis

*In this chapter Cheryl Davis approaches the process of user partici-
pation in architectural design from the viewpoint of the user, particularly the physically disabled user. For another interpretation of the
role of the physically disabled design consultant in the studio, readers
are invited to compare Cheryl Davis's perceptions, which reflect her
experiences as a political activist, with Peter Trier's discussion in chapter 7.*

When the Architectural Design with the Physically Disabled
User in Mind project began, I was working in Washington, D.C.
as program associate for the American Association for the Advancement of Science, which was sponsoring a project on the
physically disabled. For several years before that I had worked
in Massachusetts for a state agency that was developing housing for disabled people. It seemed to me that most design
professionals did not understand the range of social and behavioral factors relevant to design for disabled people. The assumption seemed to be either that disabled people, except for
dimensional requirements, were just like everybody else, or

that physical access was the sole issue. In Washington as in Massachusetts, the authenticity of consumer participation was constantly at issue. I was, accordingly, pleased to read Lifchez and Winslow's *Design for Independent Living*, with its emphases on social factors and user participation. Lifchez and I corresponded and met, and he invited me to participate in the project as an evaluator.

That users could become meaningfully involved in architectural education excited me. Many of my friends, fellow consumers, have expressed the idea that if only the needs of disabled people were somehow incorporated into the basic education of young architects, they would learn to account for them in their practice. We often said, "If only we could make you understand what we want, what we need, how we feel." Here was a chance to do just that. But my enthusiasm was tempered by my experiences with the misuse of consumer and user participation. I had seen and served on advisory committees on which the presence of consumers was purely political, required chiefly to legitimize the committee's claim that consumers were participating actively in policy making.

In March 1979 I attended the three-day project conference in Berkeley. Representatives from the five schools that were participating in the project gathered to report on their activities. As an evaluator, I found their reports depressing.

At one school the faculty member in charge of the course did not appear to believe that either he or his students had anything to learn from the consultants. From his experience in designing hospitals and custodial institutions, he presumed an expertise on the needs of disabled people, and the consultants were conspicuously superfluous. At another school, the design problem concerned a site in a remote city. This choice whetted the students' interest but denied the design consultants any direct experience or knowledge of the site. (And how the blind consultant was expected to contribute was a mystery.) At a third school, the professor seemed uncomfortable around disabled people, and he reported great difficulty in identifying prospective consultants, although several capable and conspicuous disabled individuals and organizations were operating in and around the university.

At the fourth institution the studio, on the second floor of a building that had no elevator, was inaccessible to mobility-impaired persons. While in theory consultants could have been carried in, that unsafe and uncomfortable exercise would only have taught students that disabled people are a lot of trouble, literally a burden. Instead of moving the studio or simply withdrawing from the project, the professor resorted to the blandly pragmatic recourse of using only consultants with visual impairments. I could envision an instructor asking this professor the next quarter, "Do you think you will bring physically disabled consultants into the studio again?" and he would reply, "Oh, we tried them once, but they didn't work out." No one would know why the plan had not worked, but the difficulties would be attributed, I thought, to the "fact" that "handicapped people are so poorly equipped to hold their own." The lack of authenticity in their involvement would not be cited.

In Berkeley, things looked promising. The site was reasonably accessible, the disabled users abundant, and the project director obviously enthusiastic. I was perplexed, though, by the director's apparent belief that if one combined the right ingredients, something wonderful would emerge "organically."

I was sure the consultants could make a meaningful contribution to architectural education, yet I wondered whether their involvement in these courses would be meaningful. With little or no education in aesthetics, architectural history, or structural technology, unaware of the design process and unable to read a blueprint, what could the consultants contribute to the designs? Nothing, the consultants and students might think, if they assumed that technical skills were required.

"You're the experts," the design consultants were told, but what did that mean? It seemed a hollow encouragement, offering no guide to the nature of their expertise: What did they know that students might find useful? The consultants were not experts in barrier-free design, indeed did not know a chamfer from a soffit. Unsure of their role, the consultants could only fall back on personal experience as a subject of discussion—which, in a way, was exactly what was needed. But I had been taught to value objectivity above all, and my desire to share my subjective experience of the environment had been actively discouraged. Had the consultants also learned to doubt the usefulness of their personal experience? And what about the question of privacy? More than many others, disabled people are susceptible to the demands of the casually curious to reveal intimate information, too often for no better reason than to pass the time. Not surprisingly, they tend to become reticent. To supply vivid and appropriate insights from one's own life requires a high degree of self-confidence. It takes inner security to discuss environmental needs, preferences, and experiences in effective and subjective, rather than logical and objective, ways. In the consultants' place, I would have been tempted to play the role of barrier-free design expert.

Too often, disabled people are expected to be experts on subjects such as ramps, and each is expected to act as a spokesperson for all disabled people. But what would be more useful to the student, I thought, was to describe the frustration of being unable to get to a terrific sale on lingerie or sporting equipment because the elevator was out of order, or the desire to find a wheelchair-accessible disco. It would be a revelation, I imagined, for a student to know that some people dance from their wheelchairs. As I gradually surmised, it was the sharing of experience—the trips to discos, the things people did and liked, the way they pursued their respective happinesses—that the project director hoped to elicit.

The consultants at Berkeley were intriguing people. Highly articulate and intelligent, they dropped into the discussion one thoughtful insight after another. Intensely aware of their role ambiguities, they demanded ever more clarity, more visibility, and more voice, and they got it. My fear that their presence was of a tokenist nature proved unfounded.

The concerns of the consultants were expressed in terms of power, of authority with the students—in other words, politically. How much less credible were they, relative to the instructors? Could their views matter to the students at all, when it was the instructors who determined the grades? (It seemed to rankle the consultants a bit that they lacked input on the grading, but this seemed essential to the students' trust and openness with them.) How the consultants should be introduced to the students was an important question. The relentlessly political analysis of the studio work seemed excessive, but it was necessary to validate the role of the consultants to the students and also to the consultants themselves. Unless the professor made it clear that the consultants were there for good purpose, they would not be effectively used. If the students doubted the consultants' value, their presence could provoke hostility or anxiety. Unable to establish meaningful relations with the students, the consultants would be unable to deal effectively with the discomfort their presence would create.

The instructors found the assertiveness of the consultants a challenge to their own authority—which, in a way, it was. Intelligent and conscientious, the instructors had labored to develop their own expertise. Who were these upstart consultants, anyway, to be jockeying for power within the studio? I wondered whether they would have been less defensive had the user category not been based on disability; it is hard to guess the significance of this factor. At first, the studio seemed to be full of bruised sensitivities. The emotional processes absorbed much time and energy, and more of it concerned disability than anyone liked to admit. Yet I had a sense of an immensely productive effort to clarify the role of the users in the studio. I was eager to see how it would all come out.

One thing that impressed me about the consultants—and I hoped the students were picking it up—was how different they were from each other. One benefit for the students of having a variety of consultants to meet was that they could perceive a group of individuals rather than a homogeneous, faceless mass of The Disabled. The uniqueness of each consultant was plain to me, but then, I was disabled myself and not prone to confuse people on the basis of physical condition. Months later, I was pleased to see unmistakable evidence that our individuality came through clearly, when a student described how the wheelchair-riding consultants got around in their homes. He realized that Peter could not get out of his chair unaided, but that Steve would probably feel free to slide from his chair to the floor, as he often did in the studio, and move about on hands and knees. He proposed that although I seemed to share

Steve's ability to maneuver, I would probably regard it as un-dignified and unbecoming, that my appearance was relatively more important to me than Steve's to him. The student was using his eyes and his mind, rather than stereotypes, and I was delighted. He would not likely design the same home for me and for Steve; physical needs would be weighed against other factors, such as age and temperament.

Consultants developed very individual notions regarding their duties. Dan, for example, saw himself as a human rela-tions advisor. He tried to analyze a team's group process and enable the group to function more harmoniously. How willing he was to share his personal experience was unclear to me, but it seemed useful that he was seen by the students as a person, rather than as a quadriplegic; he was more than his disability.

Simon was a challenge to any student's imagination and tol-erance for the unusual. He was severely spastic due to cerebral palsy, and it would have been easy, had he been less articulate, to stereotype him as brain-damaged, dull, and alien. Very much a "Berkeley type," Simon wore his hair long and sported a bushy beard. His speech was difficult to understand, so he wore a kind of helmet with a pointer projecting outward, which he used to indicate words and letters on a communication board he kept before him. A young woman seated beside him served as his interpreter by reading the words he indicated from the board. It was slow but no more difficult than having to wait for a foreign-language translation at a lecture. Because he was intelligent and thought-provoking, discounting Simon was difficult; once he had spoken, stereotyping him was impossible.

Peter looked like a graduate student in philosophy, which he was. His wheelchair's backrest sported a quiltwork face with a long, red tongue darting out saucily. Very professional in manner, he tended to express himself in abstract terms. He spoke little of his childhood, but seemed to enjoy sharing his present unconventional situation. Compared to his group-marriage lifestyle, the deviance of disability paled into insignifi-cance. I wondered whether the students found the marriage or the disability the greater challenge. Peter would say, "Well, all right, I can get in the door, but what if I want to go to bed with someone else in a wheelchair? How many chairs can fit into that tiny bedroom?" He shocked bourgeois sensibilities, but his honesty and directness were compelling.

Steve was intelligent, attractive, and cerebral palsied. His slow speech was understandable, provided you were willing to concentrate. After a moment, it was no more difficult than listening to a man with a foreign accent. He was very open about his childhood and adolescent experiences and very skilled at making people comfortable. I imagined he could offer a student a good understanding of the way in which an active disabled man would experience the world. His background in counseling also helped.

These consultants, having been with the project for a time, developed skill in understanding and responding to the two- and three-dimensional models, despite their initial unfamiliarity. Their sophistication did not limit their authenticity as users; it enhanced their ability to communicate their ideas and feelings about environments in terms the students could grasp. Their diversity of character and areas of interest suggested that there was considerable flexibility in the ways a user could work successfully with students. They were articulate, intelligent, and assertive people. When communications or interactions were difficult, they looked for flaws in the structure of student-instructor-user relationships before blaming themselves.

I began to gain some understanding of what it took to be a good user-consultant. The users needed to be of a certain personality type, and they also needed to be interested in the proceedings. Their contributions were livelier and more compelling when they cared. Equally important, the instructors had to believe in the value of user participation and act to validate the consultants' involvement.

In the summer of 1979, I was presented with an unexpected opportunity to learn more about user participation by becoming a consultant myself. I had already decided to leave Washington, D.C. Captivated by the quality of life afforded disabled people in the San Francisco Bay area, I moved to Berkeley. In each of the three quarters that I worked as a design consultant, my sense of what I was doing and how the students, instructors, and I interacted differed to some degree.

I began my "apprenticeship" during the summer session, a difficult time because in addition to instructors and the two other design consultants, the students were working with real clients and real needs. It was easy to feel superfluous. During the first several classes, I felt foolish but tried to look as if I knew what I was doing. Of course, the students were not quite sure what we were doing either, and the clients had no idea at all.

For much of the summer, any contact between a student and myself came only at my initiative. The clients never spoke to me and failed absolutely to respond to my overtures. My comments and queries, despite my by-no-means-negligible social skills, came to naught. I began to avoid encounters with clients toward the last half of any day that they were present.

The students were mildly responsive, although a bit anxious. They seemed unsure about whether they could ask personal questions of the consultants, whether such questions were appropriate, or whether the replies might cause both parties some pain. Sometimes they seemed desperate not to look uncomfortable. I worried a great deal about what I could share with them that would be useful to them and, in the meantime, tried to establish myself simply as a person who was nonthreatening and easily approachable. I decided to talk a little about myself, afraid all the while that I wasn't doing my job. ("You're the experts," the users were told.) But, in fact, I was. The students needed to know something about what disabled people do and how they live. I briefly described the cross-country drive I had recently made alone, and it was a revelation for students to learn that the rather sedate-looking lady in the wheelchair could do such a thing. It was also useful to them to learn how I moved in and out of my wheelchair and how I made travel arrangements. It was useful, but I was hard put to relate my knowledge and experience to their class projects, which seemed to belong to the clients.

Reviewing my inventory of expertise, I decided that I could talk about barrier-free design. I had consulted professionally in that area, and I felt it reasonable to base my claim to expertise on that. Feeling handicapped, figuratively speaking, by the novelty of my role, I grabbed at the chance to be a technical expert. I felt I needed to begin with a subject on which I was truly knowledgeable, and the temptation to "go technical" appeased my desperate wish to be a good consultant, to be helpful, honest, and warm without floundering conspicuously in a confused and ambiguous role. The approach was not satisfying. What I gave them was useful, but they could just as well have read it in a book. Later I would offer my personae as Disabled Woman, Career Woman, Poor Person, Minority Person—everything I could think of—but for a while I remained strictly in the Disabled mode, referring only to disability-related issues. Wrongly, I believed this was required of me. After a while, I feared I was appearing a bit obsessive about it, moralizing about accessibility or sounding like the local ramp inspector ("Oh, my Gawd, where's the ramp?"). It would have been useful to have been disabused of this notion sooner.

The students seemed to trust me, and gradually I felt freer about my role, more able to share my thoughts about how I would experience the models if I were moving through them. Further into the summer quarter, I shared my feelings and experiences, sometimes offering information on design details relevant to people with various kinds of sensory or neuromuscular impairments. I tried not to overdo it and I enjoyed what I was doing, but the "professional person" within me was feeling unsettled.

Working as a user-consultant required a personal relation to students, a sharing of subjective experiences not usually valued in professional or academic realms. I worried as ever about being unprofessional when I considered bringing subjective perceptions into my work. There were times when, as a result, I hesitated to talk. But one day I almost left the studio altogether when an instructor brusquely interrupted me as I was talking with a student: "You'll have to talk later; it's time for their lesson now." The "lesson," apparently, was what the instructors did; what I did was categorized as "talk." I felt stung, but knew I was also being overly sensitive.

By the time the summer ended, I had overcome most of my reticence, found the rudiments of a working style, and accepted responsibility for beginning interactions with students. The idea that students would come to the "experts" with questions now seemed amusingly naive. How could they ask, when they did not yet know what they did not know, when they did not know what we did know? How could they ask me a personal question, when most had probably been told as children that one should not even point at "that lady in the wheelchair," much less ask pointed questions? The students were burdened by a social inhibition that they could overcome only if I generated an atmosphere of comfort and mutual trust. I had to show students that I was comfortable enough to talk about anything, so that they could do the same.

In the fall quarter a new crop of students installed themselves in the studio. I set out deliberately and systematically to circulate and meet them all. They were friendly but noncommittal. I suggested that they could consider me someone safe to try out their ideas on, because although I might question and make them critically question their ideas and proposed designs, I was uninvolved in grading. I also suggested that I was comfortable talking about disability, if there was anything they cared to know, and that they could also tap my knowledge of barrier-free design. Some students responded with blank looks, but the majority were receptive.

These students were required to create imaginary clients or users to populate their projects. By imagining personalities and probable activities and interactions, they were to develop a social microcosm for which they would then create a responsive design. This projective technique revealed much of what students did or did not know about people. When they were uncomfortable or unfamiliar with a character, the biographies they invented were thin stereotypes: Sally would be described as a "typical child," Bob as a "typical war veteran," and Mary as a "typical disabled person," all with a noticeable dearth of detail.

The first scenarios, in which the characters were to interact among themselves and with the environment, were similarly bland. Few of the characters did much at all: Vic was a paraplegic war veteran who sat alone in his living room, ruminating bitterly about the things he could not do. Others said and did trivial or stereotyped things: Mrs. Smith was a seventy-five-year-old lady who had nothing to do but serve milk and cookies to the neighborhood children and reminisce in her sunset years, as the fires of life waned.

Feeling that their imaginations needed a workout, I began to propose alternative possibilities. Why was Vic in a house by himself? Why wasn't he married? Why didn't he have children and hold down a responsible job? Why wasn't he having an affair? Physically disabled clients were assumed to interact only with their environment, voicing to themselves in a self-conscious anomie appreciative statements about the openness of the floor plan as they sat alone in their wheelchairs. A wheelchair, of course, poses for a designer interesting problems of dimension and vertical circulation, but the design problems posed by other categories of disability are equally interesting and often more broadly applicable to humankind at large. Cognitive impairments, for example, raise a variety of questions about how settings can offer support and comfort while fostering the users' cognitive capabilities and encouraging their mastery over their immediate environment.

One student did attempt a scenario for a family that included a mentally retarded child. But the child was depicted as a passive and problematic entity arbitrarily placed here or there, an object who had no intentional relationship with her parents or her home. The child's bedroom was arranged to permit lots of solitary play—although real mentally retarded children need fairly constant attention, stimulation, and supervision from others. Most of the students were surprised to be asked to think of disabled people as spouses and parents, or even as employed. I began to realize that talking about myself was neither egocentric nor tangential. The students needed some firsthand reports of people unlike themselves. And so I began to use autobiographical anecdotes in the studio.

Personal anecdote was a heuristic device I might not have thought of if it were not for the scenarios and the "creative ambiguities" that held us in thrall. The combination of my desperate desire to validate my role and those evocative scenarios led us into new territory. I began to tell stories: how I went trick-or-treating on Halloween, with my sister accompanying me in order to run up the steps onto people's porches and ring the doorbells, none of which I could do with my wheelchair. The students were able to relate the effects of environment to the quality of a holiday experience for a disabled child. One vignette begot another, and I found myself turning into something of a circulating monologuist.

Personal anecdotes were also something about which students could, finally, ask questions. For the first time, they began to initiate contact. They began to find in me, as a user-consultant, something they needed, while I began to feel my presence validated. Often I could use these vignettes to suggest how different kinds of people, with different interests, abilities, or socioeconomic or cultural backgrounds, might respond to the situations they had just described. I could indicate the tremendous diversity of viewpoints and, at the same time, hint at common needs and possible design solutions.

When a number of the students began to keep journals, I did too. I began to think about the extent to which environmental considerations affect my thinking (a lot). The journal also offered me ideas for more anecdotes to see me through the quarter. For example, pondering a trip I made to an out-of-the-way stationer, I realized I had chosen it because the nearer shop was on a steep hill; I had been reluctant to push back upgrade with a manual wheelchair. For this reason, a fifteen-minute errand had taken an hour and a half. I also described the first time I had gone to a concert in Berkeley without calling in advance to see whether it was wheelchair-accessible; this impulsiveness was possible only because I had felt relatively sure that all concerts in Berkeley were accessible—anywhere else I would have had to call first. This helped me to explain to one student how disability often robs me of the chance to be spontaneous.

The students had been asked to write in their journals about an elderly person, a child, or a disabled person they had known. I decided to write about able-bodied persons I had known. To my surprise, I saw that I had stereotyped them; for instance, I wrote that "able-bodied people never look where they are going." True, I had often been in collisions with people who backed into me, oblivious to my warnings, but my ridiculous generalization led to a profitable discussion about stereotyping.

At the mid-quarter review, one student, Yuji, became aware of my difficulty in viewing the upper level of his group's model. Accordingly, he mounted a large mirror on a piece of wood, holding it at different angles at my request. Other consultants—the taller ones—found "Yuji's mirror," as we all called it, less useful than I did. At the final review, Yuji developed a tactile map of his group's model for use by a blind consultant. Not only was he the only student to do this, but he is the only one I have ever known anywhere to do this.

Some student groups were careful to keep the floor free of cardboard and wood fragments in their work areas. They maintained adequate clear space on at least two sides of their model to offer access to wheelchair users. I felt welcomed by these groups, as much by the tacit message of their housekeeping habits as by their words. Other groups littered the floor with debris. I spent less time with them and realized that I interpreted the clutter as lack of caring. I could have been more critical of their sloppiness, but I wanted to see how they would deal with me if I did not push the point.

One project featured a living room whose focal point was a piano grandly situated on a raised floor, a kind of dais or stage. One could imagine musical evenings with Helen Morgan leaning against the baby grand, bourbon and branchwater in hand, singing torch songs about all the men who had done her wrong. A tacit assumption about this space, however, and one that was probably not consciously articulated by the designer, is that people with significant mobility impairments either do not want or are unable to play the piano or to sing along with an accompanist. (Similar assumptions may explain why auditoriums and theaters that have been remodeled to provide access for physically disabled spectators remain inaccessible to physically disabled performers.)

The effects of the consultants' presence, I felt, could be seen all over the studio, and soon in the models as well. One group, for instance, populated its project with, among others, a disabled woman who lived alone. She worked—the group had overcome the stereotype of enforced idleness—but she seemed to do nothing in her spare time. "Doesn't she date?" I asked. "What does she do when she isn't working and isn't cooking dinner? Why does she have a single bed, when the other residents in the project have full size or better?" Sure enough, the paraplegic shed her drab demeanor and blossomed into a professional woman who was enjoying a satisfying relationship and campaigning for disabled rights. They made her sound feisty, passionate, full of interests, and real. The image was refreshing, considering how many students could not imagine disabled people who were anything but embittered war veterans or students.

The students with whom I most enjoyed working were those who had grown comfortable enough to talk, to ask questions, and to recognize that I had interests in life beyond disability. These were not always the same students whose work exhibited high concern for accessibility; there was no direct correlation, as far as I could see. Some projects depicted believable disabled, elderly, or minority characters in credible life situations. Wheelchair users were the most prominent kind of disabled characters, if only because their design needs were most obvious. But some students were willing to tackle the unusual. The access issues were often nicely balanced with other design constraints; in other designs, access was acknowledged but not confronted quite honestly; and in one or two projects, access was substantially denied and not discussed. These last turned out to be the work of teams whose workspaces had been most difficult for the consultants to approach, a correlation I believe to be significant.

I could see other changes as well. At the middle of the quarter, students often situated elderly and disabled people at remote corners of their sites, where it would be quiet and they would be sheltered from the demands of proximity to other people. By the end of the quarter these "vulnerable characters" would have been moved into more central locations, where they would be more involved with others.

In the winter quarter, though, I began to experience the first hint of growing stale. To sustain my interest, I began to think more deliberately about group dynamics, to probe more deeply my feelings about my personal environment, and to read books on architecture. It was not that I was trying to become a pseudo-instructor, but that I was becoming an increasingly sophisticated user. To some students I spoke a little more about barrier-free design; with others I talked more about people. Less and less did I confine my comments to the needs of disabled people. I was not seeking converts to a cause, although if the course left them more motivated to respond to accessibility concerns in their work, I was well pleased. I was more drawn to students who had grown up in small towns and had rarely met anyone who was not white, middle-class, able-bodied, and straight. To them I spoke not only about disabled people but also about black, gay, Chicano, and elderly people.

Unfortunately, I was unable to complete the winter quarter, because of illness. I would have liked to see where these students' biographies and scenarios led them. For these students did approach me and solicit my attention. Although they were still reluctant to ask some direct questions, they hinted about enough for me to gain a sense of direction. I was sorry to leave when they were finally initiating contact, but I was pleased to see how much we had gained.

Peter Trier enjoyed challenging what he called students' "bourgeois" sensibilities by displaying his unconventional lifestyle. Cheryl Davis quipped that compared to his group marriage, Peter's disability "paled into insignificance." Yet Peter also had a serious professional manner and was given to discussing abstract issues in terms that suited his role as graduate student in philosophy.

7

Dispelling Stereotypes

Peter Trier

Peter Trier coordinated the selection of design consultants for the project and served as a design consultant for several terms. At the time he was a doctoral candidate in philosophy at the University of California, Berkeley, writing his dissertation on Spinoza. He has since received his doctorate and begun his teaching career.

The design consultants chosen for the course were people who had been disabled since birth or for a considerable period of time and who had discovered for themselves a way to live independently and exercise control over their lives. We all had ongoing personal relationships, careers, and some understanding of ourselves and our situation. The students could easily see that we were active people, that we each had a distinctive personality and a social and sexual identity. Frank would talk about his theater projects, Barry was an architect, I was a philosophy teacher, and so on. As consultants to seventy or eighty students who were fairly bright but largely unfamiliar with disability, we were most effective insofar as we were able to show ourselves as we were, to raise provocative questions and respond to the students' questions, and to open ourselves up to the students as best we could.

I came to the studio as someone who had succeeded in the higher education system, as an undergraduate and a graduate student, and who had participated in community projects; I came as a physically disabled person who had dealt with able-bodied people who had had no experience with disability; and I came as someone who was concerned about the concept of community, how people could address their differences and develop a sense of common purpose and mutual respect.

I hoped to be perceived by the students not as an instance of some affirmative action program to bring disabled people into architecture, but as a consultant who posed a valid set of critical and intellectual standards for their projects. If I was a good consultant, it didn't matter whether I was disabled or able-bodied. In a logic class, for example, a student's fallacy is a fallacy whether the professor is short or tall, sighted or blind. An able-bodied instructor who is thoughtful and sensitive could produce the same kind of provocative confusion in the students' minds that I did. As a consultant, I asked students to think through carefully what they were doing, not simply to respond to my authority, my expertise, or my disability.

Our studio course was a general architectural design studio that emphasized social factors, although many students perceived it as a class in which they were supposed to learn about accessibility by meeting disabled people in the studio. But in fact the central theme of the course was the examination of one's stereotypes and prejudices about people different from oneself: the elderly and children, middle-class people and working-class people, gays and nuclear families, conservatives and radicals. The course enabled students to represent the possibility of community at the sites for which they were designing buildings. The course could have focused on the elderly, on children, or on ethnic minorities; the point was to ask students to extend themselves beyond their own cultural background. If a group of architects was to go to India to design a project, they would need to learn about India's people, history, culture, and traditions. But one can also undertake ethnographic research in one's own society. Able-bodied students can learn about disabled people's lifestyles and compensatory skills, the history of the independent living movement, the informal networks and formal organizations within the disabled community.

There are a number of ways to introduce disability-related issues into an architecture course. One could plan a series of lectures by professionals, able-bodied or disabled, who have some knowledge of physical accessibility, legal requirements and standards, and relevant hardware. Or one could invite physically disabled people to discuss their life experiences and some of the hardware issues. After the lectures, one could objectively test whether students have learned particular measurement factors and performance standards. The curriculum and method of our studio course, however, directly challenged such traditional classroom approaches. We emphasized an awareness of people rather than a mastery of facts or standards.

In our studio courses student designers worked to create environments that could support all kinds of people, and they strived to design them as well as possible in aesthetic terms, social terms, and emotive terms. Students were taught to take into account a broad complex of factors. No one lectured on specific accessibility factors; there was no explicit discussion of accessibility regulations, though interested students were referred to the relevant sources. Instead, the design consultants worked closely with the design teams, asking questions and making suggestions about a gamut of social concerns, which included disability but also a setting's suitability for older people or the nature of business-residential relationships in a multiuse project.

Our assumption was that intelligent consultants could make a valuable contribution to helping students perceive the needs and preferences of people different from themselves. This approach involved a host of risks. Particularly troubling for students were consultants whose points of view diverged substantively from the instructors'. In selecting consultants, we tried to choose people who were confident in themselves, who talked freely about their opinions and asked good questions about others' opinions, and who were openminded and interested in social interactions and people's needs. Then came the task of integrating the consultants into the course. Rather than inviting them to appear before the students on special occasions, this course used consultants from the very beginning, and they attended every class. The students slowly developed their abilities to use the consultants responsibly; they came to know us and to see our individual strengths and weaknesses as we responded to a series of questions, challenges, and pressures. As they worked on their design projects, the students made their own decisions; but because of our presence, they began to apply a new set of critical standards.

At the beginning of the semester a considerable number of students were nervous, defensive, and uncomfortable about having disabled people in the studio. In every class some students were excited from the start about working with us; they were interested in what we had to say, and they listened carefully, with open minds and open hearts. Some students immediately respected the consultants because we represented certain social values and concerns; other students had disabled friends and relatives. But all were unsure about the kinds of pressures or demands we would place on them. Some feared that they were going to be expected to accommodate a set of meaningless demands out of a guilty conscience; others became uncomfortable when they realized that they were not going to be given technical factors to memorize but would be asked to create biographies and scenarios about how people feel in various environments. And some students initially resented the idea that consultants who were not architects themselves would raise questions or make suggestions about their work.

But as we all worked together over the term, as the consultants tried to be useful—spending time on the students' projects, giving them credit and encouragement, suggesting improvements, helping them articulate what they were trying to do—their initial perceptions of us began to change. The lessons we taught, the jokes we did or didn't make, and the points we pushed all required students to reassess their presuppositions, to become more conscious of their intentions and the implications of their design decisions.

Value-laden choices frequently arose in the studio. In this course student architects could not ignore value issues by saying the design is value-neutral or by reducing a site's prospective users to lonely, isolated, paper-thin stereotypes. In this class students were required to create imaginary clients and flesh them out, allowing them to grow in ways that made sense. In creating two dozen client biographies, students could escape from "typical" clients to highly individualized, idiosyncratic ones. The students' choices of clients reflected their values, which did not necessarily agree with those of the consultants or the instructors. Some students valued intense association and commitment among people; others valued independence. Each student had the freedom to design buildings that reflected his or her values.

One of the most interesting portrayals in the class was the scenarios developed for the Castro neighborhood in San Francisco, the center of the city's gay community. In one session we were discussing a site in the Castro for which students wanted an environment that encouraged substantial community interaction and spirit, with an outdoor setting that would allow for live music, juggling acts, street parties, and so on. A question came up about how much noise or privacy the residents might want. Would they enjoy being able to see the street events taking place in front of their houses or would the events intrude upon them? We talked about the Castro as an open neighborhood to which a variety of people moved for a variety of reasons. Some residents would probably want some control over how close they become to their neighbors, some control over noise, physical proximity, contact, and so on. Others would want to be able to see what is going on and perhaps become involved in it. On occasion, most people do enjoy chatting with their next-door neighbors, or seeing joggers run by, or being near the neighborhood children and getting to know them over time.

To balance those needs in a particular urban environment involves skill. By playing out scenarios, looking at the overall design of the neighborhood, and clarifying the divergent needs of the residents, students began to discuss how to structure an environment suitable to the Castro. Their list of questions grew quickly: Why do people move to the Castro? Do they move there for proximity to work? to meet sexual partners? to meet other gay people? to have some sense of participating in a gay community? Is that community defined by physical openness about feelings? by sexuality? What can be done to support residents' values and to what extent will some values be supported at the cost of others? We talked about the conflict between residents and tourists, between gay residents' desires to feel comfortable expressing affection in public and their neighborhood having become a tourist attraction to which visitors come to gawk at the "freaks."

Initially, one group designing for a site in the Castro barely included any gay people in their scenarios, and the word *gay* came up only once or twice. Though the Castro is at least 60 percent gay, the students mentioned only two gay couples, one male and one female, and focused instead on a variety of ethnic groups, blacks and Chinese, Turkish and Vietnamese. One student used the word *weirdos* and spoke of a carnival atmosphere. But from his description the neighborhood was clearly not an enjoyable place where people had fun; rather it was a human zoo where strange people could be stared at.

The team's initial design gave everyone lots of private space; it was assumed that everyone wanted to be alone. The residents included a lonely, obese man who lived in a very secluded corner of the site and a blind child who had an isolated play area were he could remain "protected" from other people. The students seemed to assume that above all people want privacy and welcome any environmental features that enable them to avoid other people. They had not considered whether physical space could be used to further a sense of community identification and understanding. Several students giggled or made jokes about the neighborhood and its residents; these students were unable to consider seriously the characters they themselves had created.

Another group working on the Castro site at first trifled with the notion of installing various kinds of chains and bondage equipment in a disco they were planning. They were unable to think about gay people as whole human beings with a range of interests and needs beyond finding places to have sexual encounters. They wanted to design elaborate play areas around showy hot tubs, fancy settings for large sexual parties.

In these discussions the consultants' task was to raise questions, to support the students' examination of their biases and stereotypes—not to automatically criticize them, but to help them develop their abilities to criticize themselves. The consultant represented a force for change, a catalyst in the design teams' investigations. For example, one student was designing a pillow-pit for the Castro site. Another student asked, "What's a pillow-pit for?" The designer's answer was that it was for gay people, perhaps for sexual purposes and perhaps not. As the questions continued, it became clear that the student was unwilling to take responsibility for the area he was designing. He refused to define his intention: that the pillow-pit was a place for everyone to come and sit, or a spot to sit that had possible sexual uses, or a spot where gays would sit but other people wouldn't. My questions were intended to help the student clarify his own creations and ideas so that he could finally say, "These are my characters. This is my scenario, and this is the choice that my characters made. This is how they are living and thinking."

When creating their client scenarios, students' thoughts tended to focus on the physical furniture of the characters' environments—how the apartment is laid out, how residents and visitors get in and out—rather than on each resident as a parent or a friend or a person who holds such-and-such a job or has this or that hobby. The students had particular difficulty imagining a full lifestyle for older clients. The preliminary scenarios depicted older people who sat around doing nothing, having no family, friends, or active interests. These early scenarios also tended to ignore children; when children did appear, they were most often playing by themselves.

The disabled characters in the students' first efforts were depicted almost exclusively in terms of their disability and their logistical problems. Nonetheless, the students were generally reluctant to ask the consultants questions about how disabled people perform certain daily activities. They were not sure what they could ask us without offending us. May one ask a consultant how he gets up in the morning, how he uses the toilet, what he cannot do without help? Fearing that these were potentially embarrassing or hurtful questions, the students did not ask. Of course, some aspects of a client's daily routine are not particularly significant for designers, yet these are the kinds of questions able-bodied people are most curious about. Most of the students bypassed certain issues by creating clients who were paraplegics rather than quadriplegics. This choice allowed them to avoid the problems of people who need substantial assistance to dress and undress, bathe, eat, and so on.

The power of the course was that students started out with flat, bland client biographies and developed richer, more lifelike characters and situations. They learned to use their imaginations to visualize and to empathize. By working with consultants from the start, when the biographies were being developed, students had a chance to discuss different ways to view people's needs, and they worked at understanding people *before* they built their design models, before they committed themselves to a design solution that they would have a stake in defending simply because they created it.

Of course, for the consultation process to work the consultants had to achieve validity with the students as consultants, that is, as people who asked relevant hard questions, raised provocative points, seriously attended to what the students were doing, and responded openly to the students about themselves and their disabilities. Once the consultants established intellectual credibility and personal rapport, they could help students develop professionally and personally. The students then discovered changes they wanted to make in their designs, not in order to mimic some ideology of "crip power" but because what they once wanted to design no longer made sense to them in human terms. The consultant's job was to push the students to flesh out their clients' biographies, to spell out the vagaries, to explore more fully what their clients see, do, and feel.

Thus a large part of the consultants' work had little to do with accessibility per se. Certainly we answered questions about the height of a grab bar, the turning radius in a bathroom, or the gradient of a ramp. These technical standards do make a difference, but learning technical requirements is not as important to a student's professional development as learning to think about people and about the human implications of design choices. If we were looking at a site that had several steps up or down into an area, my first questions were about why the transition was designed that way. What purposes were served by the steps? What kind of people needed to negotiate them? How much were the steps used? What kinds of problems were the steps intended to solve? What would happen if the steps were replaced by a ramp? I asked these kinds of questions so that students could begin to imagine alternatives for the area that would best serve as many people as possible.

Sometimes we examined a site that could not be made fully accessible, and we discussed the implications of that. For example, in some Victorian houses the first floor can be made accessible but not the second and third floors. Despite that limitation, though, a physically disabled person could still live on the first floor or use it as a shop or office.

One of the most intellectually exciting discussions I participated in as a consultant was during a project to revamp Northgate Hall for the Journalism Department. [The Northgate project is described in chapter 12.] The question was what changes one could make in this classic shingle-style building to provide better access without ruining the building's historical style and identity. Could you put a lift in the middle of a famous hallway? Someone mentioned that of course the lighting in the building was a later addition and that all sorts of changes had been made since 1906, when the building was designed. We were trying to decide which features mattered, which ones were integral to the building's historical identity, and what kinds of changes would or would not ruin it. There was an excitement over these kinds of questions about basic premises, an intellectual excitement that transcended the particular issue of disability or access.

I liked being asked questions that were not directly related to disability, questions about children or older people, or just a simple "What do you think about this?" It was always very nice to watch a student who was excited by just having figured something out, or when students made a decision beyond what was expected or required of them. One group, for instance, had invented a paraplegic character, Bill, who was an occasional visitor. Then they decided that they wanted him to be a member of one of the families. So we started to discuss where to put his room, how he would maneuver around, what sorts of things he might want to do, and whether he could cook for himself. The students were really interested in solving those problems and pulled me in to help them create a realistic biography.

Another term a student saw me driving down the street, and he came over and asked me what I thought about the day's class. He seemed friendly, genuinely open and interested in what I had to say. Many other students would have just waved and walked by. Later in the term I was surveying his group's first model and we looked at the front entrance. I asked him why there were steps. He said that a straight-on ramp would have cut out part of a very nice front door. I asked him if he could come up with some alternatives, and we looked at several other entryways on the model and talked about the problems they might pose. For the front entrance I asked if he could envision a ramp that would come up from the side, following the incline of the sidewalk, and run up one side of the building. I pointed out that such a ramp would be appreciated not only by disabled people but by people pushing shopping carts or strollers or dollies to load or unload large, bulky objects. He asked if I thought the entire site should be accessible. I said yes, if it was possible, but his team would have to decide and work it out to meet their own standards. From that point on his team worked to devise a plan that made the site entirely accessible, and the result was an inviting environment that maintained its original design strengths.

In these studio classes, the students quickly realized that they could not just sit back and memorize what someone told them. They realized that they were going to have to think hard and try to make sense of complex issues. Their designs did not have to follow our preferences, and students often responded to questions we posed in ways we had never anticipated. The only certainty was that their designs were richer for our having consulted with them.

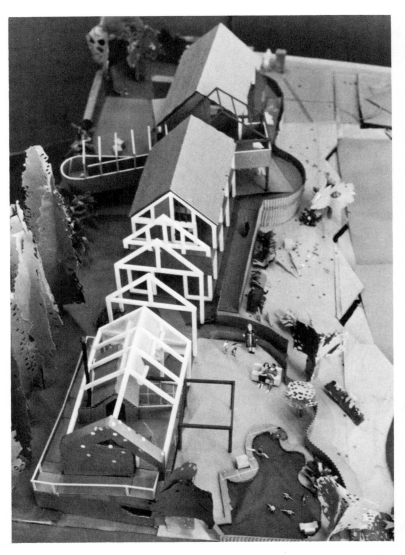

Students acquired basic planning skills in the process of working out particular examples, and they discovered "facts" through experience rather than by adhering to any given set of rules. As Lucia Howard notes, "Imagining the large-scale models and scale photographs [of clients] as full size is not difficult. The entire process seems very natural and direct." (Building design and photo by Amos Malkin)

8

Whose House Is This?

Lucia Howard

Lucia Howard and her partner David Weingarten formed Ace Architects in 1978. As a visiting lecturer, she has taught several undergraduate courses in the Department of Architecture at the University of California, Berkeley.

In 1979 Ray Lifchez invited me, as a practicing architect, to attend several reviews of his students' studio work. I was asked to represent the viewpoint of a professional who encounters in daily practice the issues raised in design courses, to assure students by my presence that access for physically disabled people was a real-life consideration, not an academic exercise. In the academic year 1979–80 I became one of several instructors for the course, and in the spring quarter I was in charge while Lifchez was on leave.

The design philosophy promoted by these classes was congruent with my own beliefs. The notion that architecture can have a subject, that it should not be abstract but literal in this pursuit, underlies my own work. In Lifchez's studios, this subject was always based on the clients themselves, their dreams, relationships, fears, and memories.

The attention to physically disabled people immediately focused the course on one conflict at the core of all architectural work: architecture as the expression of the architect's aesthetic vision versus architecture as the setting for the client's life. Both the architect and the client feel possessive of the design. Though clients seek architects whose work they like, and architects learn to be selective about clients, the competition for ownership is always at stake. When differences in values and sensibilities become too apparent, the conflict between architect and client becomes painful. Thus for the student designer the task of creating an environment for physically disabled users is an invaluable lesson in listening to others and recognizing that every client has special needs. Students learn about how life experiences vary with age, physique, income, background, family status, interests, and personality—and how their designs might reflect these experiences. At the same time they learn a great deal about their own values and assumptions.

At the beginning of the quarter, when students are asked to write biographies and brief stories about the people who will live and work in the buildings they are designing, they are compelled to relate to the clients' way of life and the building intended to support it. As the students learn to appropriate the life experience of the clients, the clients' need to identify with the design intellectually, experientially, and programmatically becomes part of the design problem. Because the student designer must begin from the clients' point of view, the struggle for ownership does not become a confrontation, and the stereotype of the all-knowing architect is effectively denied.

I was continually fascinated by the way this process elicited work based on the students' most personal feelings and values. During the lengthy project review sessions, the students revealed much about themselves and the members of their groups as they carefully pointed out features that were significant to their clients, real and imagined. Attending these reviews was always a moving experience for me, sometimes even a painful one when students revealed more than they could understand.

Initially I was rather shocked by these sessions. The more traditional design studies that had formed the core of my architectural education were based on the assumption that the training of a professional architect largely involves the development of impersonal analytic skills. Most courses convert the clients and the complexities of their behavior and specific needs into quantifiable factors, so that students need think about clients only in the abstract. For example, the many ways that people move around are translated into circulation or flow; meal preparation is reduced to the need for a triangular relationship between sink, refrigerator, and stove; and a disabled person's entire existence is represented by an 8 percent–grade ramp and a five-foot turning radius. Having mastered this shorthand for human activities, students then learn standards to accommodate certain basic forms and functions. A one-bedroom apartment, for example, will have so many square feet, depending on the market sector (rent). These standards then form the ground rules for design, and most of the students' training consists of learning to organize plans that meet these rules in ways that satisfy themselves and their instructors, and that also, especially in advanced studios, accomplish larger architectural objectives. Having learned the ground rules, students later begin to fill in the abstractions, start to look at the behavioral and idiosyncratic particularities that sometimes contradict these standards.

Lifchez's way of teaching reverses this traditional method of learning the ground rules. Rather than learning a set of abstractions that they must then tie back to their own experience, students develop an understanding of basic architectural organization from their own knowledge and imagination. Rather than designing for some vague, "average" human beings, students identify their clients and describe them in detail. Students are also encouraged to find real clients who can come into the studio for critiques. The projects are designed to fit fully imagined occasions (scenarios) realized in three-dimensional half-inch models.[1] Blocks scaled to simulate large fur-

1. A half-inch model is built on a 1:24 scale (½ inch = 1 foot). Although this may sound small, these three-dimensional models are quite depictive. In contrast, in most studio courses students work from two-dimensional eighth-

nishings and scale photographs of the clients allow students to explore tactually the relationships between people and their environment, to manipulate the furnishings and clients, and to examine how the designed spaces will be perceived and used.

The students are not consciously aware that they have learned standards. They have simply done their best to design places to support their clients' way of life. They report discovering certain facts or organizing certain spatial arrangements as the result of personal experience rather than adherence to rules they were taught. Basic planning skills are acquired through working out particular examples. Imagining the large-scale models and scale photographs as full size is not difficult. The entire process seems very natural and direct. The act of design is never dissociated from the clients; the act of design is experienced as a struggle to embody the client's way of life most fully and beautifully. Aesthetic decisions are referenced to the life within the structures, and designers and clients become joint owners of the final product.

In comparison to more traditional approaches, this class is deceptively simple. The course is designed to teach the fundamentals of architecture through direct experience rather than through abstractions. The half-inch, three-dimensional models help beginning students in visualizing the actual size of an imagined space or the components of an invented construction. Once students have acquired these skills, they can work effectively with more economical, smaller-scale models and drawings.

Ownership and Authority

When students enter their first architectural studio, the architect's absolute possession of the design is often an unquestioned axiom. These students, like the general public, often know little about the profession and harbor romantic notions

---

inch (⅛ inch = 1 foot, or 1:96) drawings, which are, at best, schematic diagrams of a building's plan or form. The small scale of eighth-inch drawings thwarts any serious discussion between students and instructors about issues of function or construction.

of what an architect is and does. They imagine the profession to be rather glamorous, though casual: Architects are, for them, artists who also possess a great store of technical knowledge, cool and unflappable managers, and connoisseurs of life. To the extent that clients enter into this romance, they are imagined as grateful and admiring.

While the protagonist described above resembles no one so much as James Bond (or perhaps Howard Roark), this dream image is to a degree shared by practicing architects. A growing body of literature on users' perceptions of architecture strongly suggests that architects too often place their personal aesthetic fulfillment above other concerns. For decades the profession has failed to perceive the disastrous results of its social myopia. Architects have now been jolted into an awareness that all people are not like themselves, and further that what works for Joe will drive Mary crazy. Recently the profession has been forced to provide for a group of people who are even more critically unlike the majority of architects than any other "disowned" group: disabled people. For most architects, thinking about disabled users is a new and relatively unwelcome experience. To think of them as co-owners is particularly difficult when the profession's prevailing image of a disabled person resembles nothing so much as a disgruntled wheelchair demanding that the world be made level.

When the students arrive in the studio with romantic images of the architect as lone champion of an aesthetic vision, the instructor's job is to cultivate a sensitivity to the client and to establish an awareness that an architect's primary role is a social one. The designer's real clients are the people who will live in or work in the buildings, not the developers or other middlemen.

When I first began to attend the design reviews, I thought the physically disabled consultants were so outrageous that even the most complacent students would react to them. One quarter Steve Hoffman, who has cerebral palsy, arrived at the first class shortly after it had begun. We had all heard a distant roar growing louder and closer, when suddenly the door to the lecture room opened and Hoffman drove in on a minimotorcycle. He parked it in the front of the room, said hello, dismounted, and crawled around to the back where his fold-up chair was attached. Refusing offers of assistance, he removed the chair, opened it up, pulled himself into it, and moved it into line with the other chairs to listen to the lecture. All this required a great deal of effort. Steve explained that because his motorized wheelchair was broken he had to use the motorcycle for transportation. His entrance made a powerful impression.

Though not all so dramatic, all our consultants were articulate and assertive; their impact was not a product only of their disabilities but of disability coupled with an open demand for fully equal rights. They would often ask extremely difficult questions. As time passed, these questions were less strictly about accommodations for disabled people and more often about other dimensions of the projects, and this change was for the good. A consultant who speaks only about the technical aspects of disability appears less credible, less vital, and less competent that one who can and will speak to the other concerns. Our consultants' diversity of interests and high level of intelligence critically affected not only what students learned but also the image they acquired of disabled people. Hidden prejudices and stereotypes necessarily falter in the presence of people who are obviously intelligent and perceptive, and who are so different from one another that they defy categorization.

Early in the project I had the uncomfortable impression that the students were being audited, that their accessibility accounts were being closely examined. The project director, the instructors, and the consultants all seemed extremely interested in tallying up the accessibility scorecards, and the tone was moralistic. Yet the students did not seem disturbed by this. Most had thought about the issues of accommodation and had anticipated these questions. Still, it is painful to watch a student try to explain to a disabled person why a certain unit or place is inaccessible, painful for both participants and observers. The student cannot make any response that is not awkward, and no consultant can avoid taking it somewhat personally.

I discovered later that one of the most difficult aspects of teaching this class is doing the accounting, which none of us likes to do anyway, without being moralistic or handing down a decree. With disability-related issues there is a certain danger of achieving exactly the opposite of what is intended. Students may find the entire subject of disability and architecture distasteful and unpleasant to think about or they may find a particular consultant distasteful. In either case, the student's empathetic response is effectively canceled. I also worried that if I disagreed with a consultant he or she might feel more undermined than would an able-bodied instructor in the same situation. Only other architects know how unlikely it is that any two people (architects or not) will respond the same way to a design issue.

Pedagogically, the design consultants are central to the basic intention of the course: to teach students how to appropriate another's life experience. The only way to test whether or not a setting will work for a disabled person is to imagine oneself to have that disability and to be in that setting engaged in a sequence of activities. The process of thinking through a disabled person's use of a place then becomes a model for thinking through an eight-year-old's use of a place or a great-grandfather's or a working mother's. The comments and observations of the design consultants thus enable students to develop a thoughtful and precise process for designing for all people. From the consultants' finely tuned insights into the physical and psychological realities of lives beyond the experience of most students, the students draw their own insights, and this internalization of another's experience will ultimately serve them better than any series of rules.

Most students at first find disability terribly frightening or terribly sad. As the course progresses, they find disability still difficult but also an interesting and absorbing design problem as well as a social and political issue. The opportunity to know the consultants, to hear their stories, their demands, and their "crip jokes," enhances students' sensibilities and genuine personal concerns. While the staff are comparatively "loud" in demanding that the needs of the disabled be thoughtfully addressed, and we sometimes demand more than "reasonable" provisions, what seems to us an overstatement is rarely so perceived by the students.

More than "Just the Facts"

Many architecture students have one feature in common: a certain yearning after the "facts." Quantifiable information that can be committed to memory is the most familiar unit of knowledge, and architecture students trust that school will or ought to fill their heads with quantities of technical data.

The format we provided for students who chose to write journals was an effort to balance experiential concerns and technical ones. At least three times during the quarter, journal writers were to answer two questions:

Tell something of the experiences you have had with any of these groups of people:

- the physically disabled
- elderly or frail people
- children
- parents with small children
- members of an ethnic minority (other than your own)

Write down at least three major design factors you would consider in designing a residence for several members of each of these five groups. Review your lists at several points during the quarter.

On the first go-around, most of the entries for design considerations for all types of people are brief and technical. For the disabled and the elderly in particular, the considerations tend to be compensatory features—ramps, elevators, wide halls, good lighting—intended to counterbalance a physical impairment or accommodate necessary equipment. They address functional needs of the first order, based on an outsider's observations; while desirable, they are motivated by the urge to compensate for deficiencies rather than to enlarge latent possiblities. For example, many students view children as small creatures who will continually try to hurt themselves and get in the way. The first group of design considerations for children included various devices for locking things up and plans for play spaces where they would not be underfoot.

As the students began to consider the life experiences of these groups, their interests shifted from compensatory to creative, from an orientation toward what cannot or should not be done to a focus on what could be done. One student's initial entries under design considerations for the disabled were a thoughtful list that met first-order functional and technical requirements: ramp and elevators; clean, well-marked, easy safety features and clear access; and adapted washing facilities. His final response to the same question was: "I read about a paraplegic who was his high school chin-up champion, and it struck me that other handicapped people I've met and seen have unused muscles in their bodies *other* than at the handicapped areas. I think it would be very good to provide special equipment so that disabled residents, if they were able, could exercise other parts of their bodies. Say, put in a special chin-up bar or sit-up area." While this is still a fairly technical idea, it adds another dimension to the residents' possibilities for living.

The journal keepers also moved from purely functional aspects to psychological considerations. One student, for example, stuck by her original list, but added two paragraphs about what these considerations meant:

Accessibility throughout space: As a disabled person, I would like to be able to go anywhere, without any barriers. This is especially important in my own realm. An apartment, a house, a studio—it doesn't matter so much what it looks like (unless I'm designing it), but that it is *home* for me. A home—my home—is a place where I'm comfortable to do whatever I please.

Sense of security, comfort: No matter what kind of handicaps I have . . . I would want to feel secure in my home. To be physically comfortable, I'd probably insist on easily accessible furniture, yet aesthetically pleasing.

Another student observed: "A handicapped child is as any child. The difference, and a major one in a child's life, is the added burden of needing or feeling the need to become at one with the norm, to conquer as much and more than everyone else. To help, one need not be obvious, but instead subtle. Designing for the elderly is just personal foresight in the human dilemma of aging."

Some students realize very quickly that disability is only one kind of special condition in someone's life. One student compared a childhood friend's disability to his own shortness:

When I was a child of seven or eight, I had a friend, Michael, also seven or eight. He was handicapped, polio, I think. It didn't really affect our friendship or drastically reduce the quantity or variety of games we could play. No, we couldn't play a real game of freeze tag or an exciting one of duck-duck-goose, but we could spend hours building block houses, castles, and bridges, or papier-mâché dinosaurs, not to mention swinging on swings or spinning around on the playground merry-go-round. The handicap didn't play an important factor in how I felt about him, or at least I don't remember it doing so. Perhaps that was because I was the smallest of all my peers, a handicap in itself, and therefore did not see a lot of relative difference between us. There were certain things he could not do, like threading a needle, and other tasks I was unable to do, such as pulling the screen down over the blackboard before the showing of a movie in the second grade.

One of my most vivid memories of childhood was selecting a present for Michael's eighth birthday. My mother took me shopping. I wanted to get him some of the missing dinosaurs from his set or new matchbox cars, the VW bus and Mercedes convertible. But my mother steered me away from these choices; she wanted something more challenging, more therapeutic, if you will. An erector set was the final selection. Today I view this choice as a fabulous one and admire my mother greatly for it.

As this journal entry demonstrates, students can learn both to enter the life experiences of another and to realize how much of a role an architect's own background and values play. Early on in the course we read a brief article by John Cheever, "The Second Most Exalted of the Arts," in which Cheever claimed "from one look at the Kaufman house in Pennsylvania I knew Frank Lloyd Wright's shoe size." I asked the students what they thought this meant. Most were puzzled, though some knew or guessed that Wright was short in stature, and that his buildings betray this in their scale.

Learning to see the world through the eyes of someone who is disabled can be a revelatory experience. The environment suddenly loses its neutrality and is revealed as a protagonist. The most ordinary elements acquire significance, and students become aware of aspects of the environment they have never noticed. Achieving psychological comfort, making someone welcome, supporting certain interactions, or allowing a graceful retreat—all these activities acquire physical reality.

In this way, disability-related issues serve to teach a mode of thought that is critical to good design. Students cannot be told to design from another's point of view; they will pursue this method only if they find it necessary. Those who do not feel the need to understand the relationship between the environment and a way of life may never rid themselves of the notion that design is only a formal and technical exercise that must satisfy certain programmatic requirements. Such students will become architects who will be eternally frustrated by clients' demands for ownership, for a design that suits their needs and not just the architect's aesthetic.

As a practitioner, I find that working with the design consultants has affected me in two ways. First, the building code requirements are now far more comprehensible because I have walked beside disabled people and seen the difficulties posed by doors that swing the wrong way, steep gradients, and phones that are too high. More importantly, the manipulations involved in planning for access no longer seem dry technical requirements, and physically disabled users are no longer an abstract population. Instead I can visualize people I consider friends, who have the same needs as able-bodied people plus a few more. The technical requirements cease to be an imposition once the imaginary wheelchair is occupied by someone I know.

The success of the course rests on its provocativeness. By establishing a humanistic basis for design, the course provokes students to interact, react, absorb, create, and defend, to draw on their own resources so that what is learned is also experienced. The large models are the tangible artifacts of this process. Having learned to build from the clients' concerns and to work through a complex project with three or four teammates, students are equipped to handle creatively the ever-present issue of ownership. The technical aspects of accessibility become meaningful because students have a personal motive for making their buildings accessible: They want Cheryl Davis or Steve Hoffman to be able to fully enjoy their creations. By moving throughout a proposed building with Cheryl or Steve in mind, students also discover weak points that the codes may not anticipate.

Architectural Richness

The course has sometimes been criticized because it teaches design for particular clients rather than for a wide spectrum of potential inhabitants. But in my view this is its greatest strength, for standard clients or projects, average families, and typical sites do not exist. The exercise of designing for an average population is one that often leads to average design. The lowest common denominator wins out.

If beginning students are misled into believing that the strength of a design is independent of human circumstances, it is difficult for them later to relate architecture to the human experience of claiming and occupying a building. Yet there is a great need for architects to learn how to make claimable buildings. The modernist aesthetic has produced vast numbers of buildings that proclaim "hands off" to the public, buildings that are standoffish and unknowable, both emotionally and physically. As a result, most people feel disowned by the buildings they work in, live in, and shop in. Filmmakers and novelists use the image of the modernist landscape to symbolize alienation and estrangement. In response, many architects and clients are now demanding buildings that are more meaningful, that offer a human scale and an imaginative foothold. The challenge in design is to create structures that involve and reflect individual clients while also affording possibilities for reinterpretation by future users.

The word we use to describe what we are seeking is *richness*, and richness in a design results from an architect's intense human involvement with what is being designed and who it is being designed for. The participation of physically disabled consultants in the studio course affords students an involvement with surrogate clients, which enlivens their designs and produces work animated by a powerful and heartfelt concern for the psychological and physical well-being of their clients. Students often discover the hollowness of their presuppositions about other people's way of life, as they learn to pay attention to the subtleties of other points of view. The telling and embellishing of stories about the imagined residents and the site fills the project with life, and students enjoy imagining ways to design buildings that inspire still more stories, more life. The construction of three-dimensional models provides an immediate medium for visualizing the implications of issues and facilitates the discussion of spatial ideas that are hard to verbalize. The students work in easily understandable space, and are less likely to be confused later by the two-dimensional deceptions of architectural drawings. Through the layering of these many techniques that create involvement, the course acquires tremendous richness.

Though one may end up becoming an advocate for accessibility, this course finally does not seem to be a course about design for the disabled. In the later stages of the design reviews, both consultants and staff approached disability-related issues as one of many integral concerns, not necessarily the predominant one. Students thereby come to feel that the concerns of disabled users are fundamental considerations in design, not special criteria. And that is as it should be.

At the beginning of each term, Steve Hoffman probably occasioned the most nervousness among students; yet he usually won almost everyone over with his infectious humor and his patience. "I've seen him sit for hours quietly listening as a student pours out his problems, never taking his beautiful eyes from the student's face," Wendy Sarkissian observed.

9

"The Vitalizing Challenge Of Dissonance"

Wendy Sarkissian

Wendy Sarkissian participated in our project as an outside observer during one of the two years she spent at U.C. Berkeley as a visiting foreign scholar. Here, she candidly describes her apprehensions about the project; in chapter 10 she draws on her observations about the students. She is now a practicing social planning consultant in Sydney, Australia. With Clare Cooper Marcus, she is the co-author of Housing As If People Mattered *(University of California Press, 1986).*

A student is telling her story, and a small group of people, some in wheelchairs, are clustered around to listen:

I'm Michelle, I'm twenty-four and I'm a jazz piano player, and I've been going to private schools for the blind. But then my parents thought it was time I got out into the world. I'm kind of introverted, so I started to play the piano. I have a kind of natural talent for it and I practice at it . . . and I couldn't . . . didn't want . . . to talk to other people. So I got out of school and joined up with a jazz group. Now I'm beginning to talk to people more.

Q. Do you live by yourself?
A. No, I live with Susan Hiller. She's about my age. She works in a nutrition store. We have a one-bedroom apartment, and I have a baby grand piano downstairs. I've gotten into writing music now.
Q. Really? How do you write music?
A. With great difficulty!

The young student laughs and throws up her hands in mock despair. I have to laugh, too. She's not blind. Nor a pianist. She's an architecture student imagining herself to be one:

I have a guide dog. I don't need an attendant really. Everything I have is very set, and my roommate does the cooking and everything like that so I really don't have to worry: Everything's pretty much taken care of. And my jazz group kind of takes care of me. When I go to practice they pick me up.

Q. Have you been blind since birth?
A. Yes.
Q. What are the implications for designing for you if you've never seen anything?
A. Well . . . I haven't really developed that as much as I'd like to yet. One of the things I like when I play the piano is warm sun. It feels good. I like very uncomplicated furniture because I don't want to go tripping around everywhere. And I have to set out my music so it's easy for me to figure out where everything is.

At the next low table, Thom and Nancy spin the tale of a young Vietnam veteran:

We have a guy who was injured in Vietnam during the war. He's an American Indian; his name is Roy Clearwater. He's very congenial, kind of a rowdy guy. He zips around in his electric wheelchair all the time. And he has a lot of friends who come over to visit him a lot. He plays darts in our bar.

Q. What's the nature of his disability?
A. I can't visualize how his body looks in his wheelchair. That means I haven't gone that far with it, but his arms and upper body are still very alive and active. There would be something about his legs, that they just aren't usable.
Q. He's paralyzed from the waist down?
A. Yes.
Q. Does he have a specially modified apartment?

A. Yes. But he still . . . thinks that, when people come in, he doesn't want the apartment to be looked at differently than anybody else's. He still wants to feel like, well . . . maybe at some point . . . well, maybe next year he'll be able to walk around again: that it's not just that "this is it and I'm stuck this way for the rest of my life."

He lives alone; he likes to live alone because he was always a really independent guy. He got injured and it really threw him for a loop for awhile. He either works at CIL [Center for Independent Living in Berkeley] or he used to work there for awhile. He's young—about twenty-eight; he's out a lot, and he doesn't eat much at home: he doesn't need a big kitchen. And he goes to the pub a lot. He's actually a very friendly person. He knows everyone there and he's friends with everyone there. They like him and he likes them—kind of a certain "center" in terms of warmth or something.

Q. Does he drive?

A. I haven't thought of him driving. Obviously he could drive. Cheryl can drive.

From her wheelchair Cheryl Davis smiles in agreement. Certainly she can drive. She's just driven her modified van from Washington, D.C. to Berkeley to participate in the Architectural Design with the Physically Disabled User in Mind project. Cheryl is one of four physically disabled consultants participating in the project. She's thirty-four, an admitted intellectual with a taste for philosophy. She was a Loeb Fellow at Harvard, where she teaches one course a year, and has in the last ten years acquired a distinguished résumé in the field of disabled people's rights and barrier-free design. She is outgoing and talkative; the students warm to her immediately. Cheryl uses a wheelchair; she has spina bifida and has been disabled since birth.

Steve Hoffman is with another group at the end of the studio, but I can hear his laughter and catch sight of his wild gestures from the corner of my eye. He's younger than Cheryl, and as outgoing and uninhibited. Counseling is his field of expertise: I've seen him sit for hours quietly listening as a student pours out his problems, never taking his beautiful eyes from the student's face. Steve has worked in this course for several quarters now. He buzzes around in an electric wheel-

chair, frequently in the company of two or three of his housemates. He speaks with difficulty and I find him very hard to
understand at first. He has cerebral palsy and has difficulty
controlling his muscles—and his infectious laugh.

But Steve's disability does not keep him from communicat-
ing; to the contrary. In one of the early lecture sessions, I recorded the following observation: "Steve appears to be gestur-
ing for attention. After several false starts, the message is
delivered: Being able to be self-critical is a necessary tool in any
profession. 'Be detached,' he admonishes, 'but also rely heavily
on your team members, for along with being detached you *must*
be dependent on other people. The more people are dependent
on one another, the better.' "

Peter Trier is the philosopher of the group, a doctoral student in philosophy who holds his head so erect on his long
neck that he could be directing a class on posture or decorum.
Peter has been working with Ray Lifchez for years; nothing that
happens in the class seems to surprise him. Many times during
the quarter I am impressed by his carefree questions and precise analysis. He reveals little about his life, but sometimes
when I enter the studio a young woman in green tights is sitting on his lap. Like Steve, Peter operates an electric wheelchair. He has a degenerative disease that leaves him without
strength in his muscles; this contributes, I suppose, to his
rather fragile and ascetic appearance.

We did not see much of Jane Carpenter this quarter. Teaching
and single-handedly raising her four-year-old daughter kept
her from the studio more than we had hoped. When she came,
I was impressed immediately by her close attentiveness, which
made me more aware of her blindness. She would stand, perfectly silent, with her head cocked as a student explained the
rationale for a design. When the student finished, Jane would
fill the studio with her vivid imaginings of how it would be to
live in that house. Soon everyone was chatting animatedly. My
notes during the first studio session read: "Ray places the map
on the table in front of Jane. She feels it gingerly, lightly touch-
ing the tops of the paper spirals and pinned-on notations. Carefully, he takes her hand and guides it around the perimeter of

the map, explaining each part. We are all engrossed and perfectly silent. Ray helps Jane feel the second map. Then her questions begin: 'Do you think a shy person would feel comfortable here? It feels very exposed to me.' "
These four remarkable people are my new colleagues.

Expectations and Fears

I was delighted to be invited to work as an observer for the fourth quarter of the Architectural Design with the Physically Disabled User in Mind project, and I hoped that my years of teaching social aspects of architecture would help me along. And I was curious. In a little over a year at Berkeley I had heard a great deal about the course and the project. Some described the class as a gigantic encounter group. To others, it was the place to learn precise skills for building the splendid three-dimensional models displayed in the school's hallways every quarter. Or a social-factors course, supposedly the college's forte. Former students recalled a marathon, with prizes going to those who survived the most all-nighters. Everyone had an opinion.

The assignment suited my own interests well. In the past year I had been introducing barrier-free design in my social-factors course in the Department of Architecture and Landscape Architecture. I had developed a close friendship with a severely disabled graduate student and had returned from a 2,700-mile journey in her modified van. My consciousness had been raised to the point that I saw barriers everywhere, and too often I despaired of ever finding workable solutions. The cynicism of some of my students discouraged me; the "conversions" of others inspired me. Not being an architect, I was eager to learn how an architect's way of teaching barrier-free design would differ from my own.

With this mixture of emotions, I attended the first meeting with my colleagues: four physically disabled consultants and five able-bodied instructors. I was acquainted with one of the instructors, but all the consultants were strangers. I had never been introduced to a blind person until I met Jane or spoken to anyone with cerebral palsy until I met Steve. I had to ask Cheryl what spina bifida was, and I shared the students' curiosity about the causes of Peter's particularly fragile appearance but was too shy to ask him.

My initial impression was that a great stew of instructors, disabled consultants, and students was to be stirred up in the sixth-floor studio. And, in a manner not fully understood by the magician himself, time would work its predictable magic: Students would absorb from the rich broth everything they needed to know about barrier-free design, from politics to standards and regulations, and would emerge committed to making the world accessible. But as the weeks progressed and the emphasis of staff meetings changed from planning to feedback, I began to realize that I was monitoring a carefully structured process in which experiences were orchestrated to enable students to develop a set of progressive skills, each building on the previous one.

I had a rather long list of other concerns. I feared that the emphasis on disability issues, particularly codes and standards, would turn students off—I had seen that happen before. The speed of the quarter (too long when I was a student; now too short for the teacher) did not allow much time for students or consultants to work through feelings about the project or each other. Some of the experiences could be threatening, and I wondered who would be there to hold everyone's hands. The combination of threat and reaction (flight or fight?) and the intense pressure to finish and produce a good model also worried me.

And, of course, I had my own feelings to handle. Here were four articulate, experienced "crips" who knew more about this subject than, fates willing, I would ever need to know. I expected them to be articulate, and they were. (Cheryl had me terrified for weeks.) I assumed they would be aggressive about disability issues, able to launch without hesitation into the impromptu speeches I had come to expect from academics. Each one, I imagined, must have a pat lecture up his or her sleeve, facts and figures for ammunition at the ready, and materials to distribute, sign-up lists and petitions entreating legislators to remove social and architectural barriers. I expected each one to be walking (or rolling) yellow pages of referrals on all related matters, to bring other disabled folks into the studio or take us on field trips, to provide access to local and national resources. I supposed we would all be socializing together (consistent with the stew hypothesis), and that some of them would join the midnight marathons in the studio as the quarter came to end.

I did not expect these four to become involved in issues not related to accessibility. Nor did it occur to me that they would participate in assigning grades. For some reason I expected Steve, Peter, Jane, and Cheryl to speak with one voice, presenting a united stand on most issues. Although I was accustomed to lecturing about barrier-free design, in their presence I felt uncomfortable about the limits of my new-found expertise. Of course my experience was limited: Was it audacious to presume that *I* could speak for *them*?

No wonder I was afraid. Later I heard students repeat, almost word for word, my own fears. Trying my best to be a dispassionate observer and a good interviewer, I could only respond, "I can understand where you're coming from."

Let me give an example, from my observation notes on an early lecture class.

I am sitting in front of Peter and Steve during the slide presentation. My hunch is that they have decided that this is the day to shock us dramatically into a realization that they are sexual beings. Peter is flanked by two very affectionate people: a woman in dramatic green tights and a man, rather heavily made up. Both are paying him attention—intimately. Steve also has a woman on his knee. The demonstration by Peter and his friends continues after Ray finishes showing his slides. The woman and the man are both caressing Peter and he's looking on blissfully. I'm wondering if it is really appropriate for him or them—or any of us, for that matter—to behave that way in a class. A student sitting in front of them shifts uneasily and looks around her. I feel very uneasy.

I was also fearful of being overly solicitous, too helpful, opening doors for people who did not need help. The first time I asked Cheryl whether I should push the elevator button for her, she sharply reminded me that she had two good arms. I was terrified of being stereotyped as a "crip camp follower" who salved her conscience by working on a disability project. Although I could demonstrate a longstanding commitment to the reform of architecture, I was, as my disabled friend termed it, a tenderfoot as far as disability was concerned. When one of the consultants proclaimed, "You walkies are all the same," after I had given directions that caused delay and inconvenience, I smarted with rage and shame for weeks.

My role in the course was ambiguous. I frequently sat in lectures and studios, taking notes and photographs, but I could not offer opinions and I was not (or did not feel like) a full voting member in staff meetings. The passive and dispassionate role I was expected to play was difficult for someone used to being active and expressing opinions.

These professional and personal concerns were exacerbated by a more mundane but equally awesome difficulty: I could not understand Steve's speech. Try as I would in the early days, I still missed over half of what he said. In lectures I often turned to a nearby student for a translation or waited for an instructor to pick up on his comments and summarize them.

Realities

As I could have expected, few things about the course went just as I had expected. None of the consultants gave prepared lectures. An important part of their participation consisted of chiming in, usually in support of an instructor. Steve did this most often and quite effectively. In the third week he delivered his passionate homily about the need for all of us to be dependent, and later he delivered an impassioned plea for a more realistic approach to the imaginary clients. "Show us their *unattractive* side," he pleaded; he'd had enough of "soap operas." Peter spoke in lectures as well, but because his speech is not impaired one does not have to concentrate so carefully and be absolutely silent to understand him. (Steve clearly has an edge over everyone in that respect.) Also, Peter talks like the scholar he is; he does not sound very different from the instructors, and by the end of the quarter, lectures by instructors got short shrift.

Understandably, poorly resolved issues of access brought strong reactions in the final reviews. At one review Cheryl reacted vehemently to the lack of a ground-level bathroom in a model for a therapist's home office. She pointed out that the inaccessibility of mental health facilities is a serious problem for disabled people. The student replied that she had not expected the therapist to have clients come to her home. Cheryl responded by mentioning a therapist she knows who had to move when he found he had three "wheelie" clients. Earlier in the week Cheryl had admonished another group for emphasizing vertical circulation in a house without seriously considering how a vehicle like a wheelchair actually moves through space.

Sometimes a consultant's contribution to a weekly staff meeting resulted in the introduction of new material in a lecture, a handout, or feedback to students. With so much going on, it was hard not to pick up useful information. As one student explained: "Some people think the final test was whether or not you could fit someone in a wheelchair into a place. But I don't think that was the case at all. That's where Cheryl was really helpful. I overheard her talking one day about not having mirrors above a sink that slant downward because she sometimes just wanted to be able to see herself from the neck up and forget the fact that the wheelchair started from the shoulders down. That got me thinking."

The consultants commented on many issues other than disability and access. In the first design reviews, I noted that Steve was keeping an eagle eye on vague areas in the students' thinking and in the models. With one group he discussed concerns about "surveillance," that people should be able to see their neighbors coming and going. He pointed out the unclear functions of some spaces and declared one of the invented clients to be a schizophrenic creation.

That same day I overheard Peter taking almost a devil's advocate position on a ramp for a disabled veteran. The ramp cut off sunlight from the neighboring windows, he protested, and he expressed skepticism of "overkill" solutions to access problems. The same ramp, which had not been refined to meet

Peter's requirements, came under his attack on a final review: "The way it is now if you're able-bodied, there's a tendency to say 'the god-damned ramp system.' " A visiting critic commented that the ramp made for a long walk if a resident was carrying groceries.

Humor, especially the ability to laugh at oneself, worked wonders. When a student shyly commented to Steve that she had trouble understanding him, his riposte was, "If you cannot understand what I'm saying, just ask me again. Sometimes *I* don't even know what I just said." Cheryl used humor well, too, the humor of a self-effacing storyteller: "I joke mostly because I know it will lower people's anxieties." She explained to me that through anecdotes she has been able "to suggest things to people so that they don't feel spoon-fed." A skilled communicator, she explained her method to me:

I tend to use the models as jumping-off points for other experiences. If they're asking me about an elevator, I might talk about elevators I have been stuck in and what elevators work better than others and why. Then I'll tell some funny elevator stories and move on to other topics that relate to vertical circulation. For instance, I'll talk about a time that I had to go up the stairs on my ass because there wasn't an elevator. By creating a series of images, I can give the students a chance to imagine what things feel like and look like. Those feelings, my own and the ones my stories evoke, give the students more motivation for providing alternative access for people with different abilities and needs.

Of course, there were problems, one of the most serious being the students' reluctance to ask the consultants for help. Some were naturally shy, others unsure how to ask (or, more basically, what to ask). They often seemed to expect the consultants to take the initiative. And as the quarter progressed, students got involved in building their models. At that stage, when pressures increased to finish the models, everything else took second place for most students.

Students were also sometimes perplexed when contradictory views were expressed by consultants, instructors, and visiting critics. Though the Irish stew hypothesis was based on "the vitalizing challenge of dissonance" (to use Lewis Mumford's phrase), some students were defeated by the challenge, bewildered by the expression of differing points of view. When I asked one student how his designs had changed, he explained:

In the five or six residential spaces I've designed, making something split-level has always seemed a nice way of doing things, a nice transition. But all of a sudden, that's out. Ray came over to us and said, "Well, it doesn't mean that split-level is out: it means that you have to *think* about it." But then Cheryl came over and said, "Nope, split-level is out. Forget it. No split-level. Don't even think the word." And I said, "Okay, I'll take your word over Ray's." Now, usually I resolve disagreements by doing what I think is best. But in this situation, I had the strong impression that Cheryl knew a hell of a lot more about what she was talking about than Ray did.

In short, students, like the disabled consultants, are not a homogeneous group, and they need help in dealing with their feelings. One cannot expect able-bodied students' prejudices, fears, or discomfort to disappear in one semester. But they had made a start, and I had, too.

A student helps Jane Carpenter, a blind design consultant, survey a model by guiding her hand over the cutouts and explaining each part. Some students were quite innovative in making their designs accessible to all the consultants. At least once a semester, though, a design team would mount a slide presentation.

10

How the Students Saw It

Wendy Sarkissian

As noted in chapter 9, Wendy Sarkissian served as an outside observer. Her account of students' responses to the course focuses on the ways in which students related to, or avoided relating to, the physically disabled design consultants. This chapter incorporates her in-class observations, unstructured interviews (lasting from thirty-five to ninety minutes) with one-third of the class (nineteen students) and with three consultants, and her reading of students' journals.

Engaging the Consultants

Each consultant worked with students according to his or her personal style and interests. On average, each consultant was present for six hours a week (the class met for ten hours over three days), and at any time at least two consultants were engaged in conversation with members of different design teams. The consultants were not assigned to teams but moved freely, especially at first, asking questions, volunteering information or advice, and developing contacts. Cheryl recalled: "People didn't start asking me to come over to their groups

. . . until I started moseying in and then all of a sudden it started happening. And I noted it and recorded it in my journal when it happened: 'Gee, two groups asked for me today; I suddenly feel useful.' And I realized that I had 'primed the pumps' the week before."

In the course of one meeting with a team, Jane interwove the personal and the objective:

On the bus she starts up an interesting conversation with the driver so that he or she will remember to tell her when her stop comes.

Her daughter is outgoing and has adapted to her mother's blindness, likes bringing her things to touch.

Jane likes sensual things: waterbeds, music, fireplaces, and bubble baths.

She likes to cook—uses Braille cookbooks and magnetic labels on cans.

Sometimes an instructor asked a consultant to come over to a group to lend a hand. When several were present, an active interchange of ideas usually followed:

Ray points out that we always end up with the elderly people and the disabled people living alone on the ground floor. "In future studios," he says, "we'll assign them to live *with* people." Ulysses [a student] reminds him that the house is for a *real* client, who liked the ground floor. Cheryl replies that part of the architect's responsibility is to provide alternatives. Steve expands on the need for a "two-way relationship" between client and designer, which should be more than just the client "giving you the data." Then Steve asks again about the size of the closet.

Often a simple point gained emphasis when supported by one of the consultants' anecdotes: "Ray directs the discussion to show that it will be necessary to have the central services on the ground floor. Cheryl mentions a disabled friend of hers who was forced to leave a friend's house because the bathroom was inaccessible." Sometimes students called in the consultants to provide guidance, to clarify a point in a reading assignment, or to help with the development of a client biography or scenario. Students also frequently called in consultants to resolve disagreements. Students usually responded to the consultants' initiatives by stopping what they were doing and talking a while. Often an instructor facilitated the interaction by referring or deferring to the consultants. Some students became involved with the consultants outside of the classroom. Louise described in her journal a tour that she and Cheryl had made of the inaccessible women's washroom:

Mirror above head level—too high for people in wheelchairs.
Door wings in—not against wall—dangerous for people in wheelchairs.
More than half-inch drops (not beveled) cause wheelchairs to tip.
Sinks too high; "turn" handles (on sinks/doors) should not turn but should be pushed.
Towel dispenser and tampon dispenser should be lower.
Stalls for wheelchairs should be large enough for side transfer and easy door closing.

Another student borrowed a wheelchair and tried a simulating exercise with Cheryl.

Some students modeled their imaginary clients after the consultants. "Becky Glassman" was modeled on Cheryl; during the final review of Becky's apartment, I noted: "The bottom apartment is for Becky Glassman. She's paralyzed from the waist down. She lives alone. Cheryl comments, 'Ah, but she does have a large bed; she's not always alone.' The discussion moves to floor levels: Cheryl assures us that she (and a person in an electric wheelchair) could manage a six-inch rise with a wedge of wood. She explains, using her own apartment as an example."

Part of the students' experience in getting to know the consultants was beginning to see disabled people as real people rather than objects or a homogeneous group. Sue expressed her move from generalizations to an understanding of individual needs: "In design you have to consider that it's hard just to take an average disabled person. Some people in wheelchairs can do different things. Steve—he's strong, but he has no control over his strength; Peter essentially has no strength but he does have control. So they can do very different things."

Accommodating the Consultants

Although only relatively few students felt that they were actively engaging the consultants, most found ways to accommodate them in the studio and in their designs. Some of the students' reluctance to make contact was clearly related to practical issues: How does one explain a map to a blind person? How does one talk to a person in a wheelchair (sit, stand, kneel, crouch)? How does one make room for wheelchairs in an overcrowded studio? Some students developed thoughtful solutions; as Alan explained: "A lot of people stand over Cheryl and look down. So all of us try to sit down or kneel, to get down to her level, and get real close, about the same proximity that we are here [he gestures to me], or maybe a little closer. It seems to work really well. But you can't do that with groups of seven people. How you do it at that scale, I really don't know." One group placed their model on a box close to the floor so that Cheryl could easily see it from her wheelchair. Another group used a mirror to show her the "inside" of the mapping. Bill made a topographic model of the site, labeled in Braille for Jane, but the next team to make a presentation used slides to illustrate the interiors of the buildings as they described them.

Design Strategies

By coming to know the consultants, students soon discovered that disabled people know what they need in their environment and can often, in fact, specify their needs so clearly that they make ideal clients. Sue noticed this throughout the quarter:

Cheryl's really in tune with her needs, and in tune with what she can do and what she can't do. It's really amazing. Or I could just say to Steve, "How do you feel about this?" and he'd tell me what he can do and what he can't do. He knows very well. They're both very easy to work with, much easier than someone like me who says, "Well, I don't know; I don't know what I need." I'd have to live there awhile and find out what worked and what didn't. I couldn't just say before I moved in just how I functioned. But Steve and Cheryl are so in tune with what they can do that they know right away how they feel.

Some groups devised ingenious ways to test whether their designs were barrier-free. Sue, for example, described the following method to calculate the turning radius of a wheelchair: "I made these little wooden wheelchairs to scale, and rolled them through to make sure they could work. And then Bob took up a five-foot circle and put it in the bathroom to see if it would work. We also asked Cheryl how she got on the toilet, and she showed us." Another successful design included a hot tub and sauna, with the locker room at the same level as the deck, allowing disabled people to use the hot tub along with everyone else.

Ramps, however, sometimes became a key point of contention. Many of the teams used ramps or systems of ramps to make their buildings accessible. But during the final reviews the instructors made sure that attention to access issues did not dominate the designs. Some students understood the message: Access was one issue among others that had to be considered; but other students were frustrated by what appeared to be a shift in emphasis. Tsuji devoted his last journal entries exclusively to the ramp issue, which had greatly frustrated him:

Frustrated with this project because of the varying feedback we were receiving from the different instructors: Lee liked the idea of the ramp if we could design it "right" and it would work right, but Ortha said to "kiss the ramp goodbye." These differing suggestions were a bit discouraging, but our group decided to stick with the ramp and design it well.

I thought the ramp turned out pretty well; we decided that this feature would be a very important item of our project. Lee commented that it does work pretty well; however, there could be a lot more design work done on it. Peter seemed to think the ramp worked well, and I was glad to hear him say positive things about the ramp because the main purpose of the ramp was to make the second-floor units accessible to disabled people. We also wanted to tie the ramp in with the rest of the site and not have it sticking out like a giant object placed in the middle.

During one final review Lee asked about the residents whose apartments would be entered off a long ramp: "How would you feel sitting at your living room window and watching people go along that ramp?" The conversation moved to the possibility that skateboarders might use the ramp, which was located in the interior of the apartment complex. At this point Steve came to the students' rescue, arguing that he would expect that the people who would be passing by his window would only be a "couple of near neighbors." Peter commented that it would be "an enjoyable ramp to ride up" because of its changes in height. Nearly forty minutes later, the group was still discussing the ramp. Ortha observed that the ramp did not fit the articulation of the buildings. One team member then admitted that each student had been expected to take responsibility for the part of the ramp that ran outside his or her part of the site. It didn't work, he sighed, but they wanted the ramps because elevators break down.

Other design decisions also revealed close attention to the needs of disabled people, even though they were not completely successful. Tomás, for example, carefully designed an apartment for an elderly woman with the intention that it could be easily converted for a physically disabled resident. He located it on the first floor, decided against a sunken living room, and installed grab bars in a spacious bathroom. Cheryl complimented him on these accessibility features but used Tomás's cutout of a wheelchair to demonstrate how a "fat friendly column" in the middle of the living room would block access.

Sometimes accommodation took the form of creating a less crowded environment, as in Stella's case: "I remember when we went to the Buttercup Cafe, and Cheryl saying, 'I just can't go in there when it's crowded.' But when I was in there alone I thought, 'Oh, this is nice and cozy.'" In other cases, students found that the need to accommodate people in wheelchairs helped them to order their priorities: "The house that I was thinking of designing—I sort of like split-level, sunken living rooms, and things like that. On second thought, I decided that that's just one of those preferences; it's not really that important. If it were a choice between having someone in a wheelchair being able to get around or me having my sunken living room I'd rather have it accessible."

Some accommodation took the form of mixed use: locating apartments over shops or workplaces, so that residents would be able to shop and work near their homes. To be sure, in some cases accommodation was overdone. In a few instances whole complexes were dominated by gigantic ramp systems and some apartments were so accessible that they lacked any sense of privacy or coziness. But many of these weaknesses can be explained by the fact that this was, for most students, the first design studio. Mary, reflecting on her changed awareness, regretted that it took so long to develop:

Before I came to Berkeley I was totally unaware of barrier-free design and how inaccessible buildings, streets are to wheelchair users. If I wasn't in architecture, I don't think it would have been brought to my attention. It's just not something that comes up in everyday conversation. But now I walk up and down streets looking at window styles, entrances, all of the details that I tried to incorporate into my house, even balconies. It's amazing the variety that you come across.

Priscilla also found that the course opened her eyes to the architecture around her:

I never realized how inaccessible everything was. Those things aren't just brought up everyday. I really started looking out for things when I was walking around; looking out for whether someone who's disabled could get into that. I guess I never thought about how they got into buildings. I was amazed, because you just take it all for granted. Inaccessibility is just one of those hidden things.

For some of the students the course provoked a new direction, a new commitment, in their work. Louise wrote in her journal:

My roommate asked me the other day if I would continue to design with handicap access after Architecture 101. My answer was automatic—"of course." After this class I can't imagine designing anything without confronting the issue of accessibility. It has become an important design criterion along with many others. I feel the thought we've put into accessibility has familiarized us with many possible solutions, but we also realized the difficulty of making all units accessible. These issues will enter into my designing from here on. In fact I now find it hard to believe it's been overlooked for so long!

Jan found Erving Goffman's *Stigma* a powerful influence; after reading it, he concluded that "a large part of architecture is the ability to sympathize with people and love them." From sympathy he moved to empathy:

It's difficult to realize what stigmatized people have to go through: the trauma of having to place oneself in a group of imperfect human beings, to realize that you have lost your luck and beauty, to always have the stigma be the primary identifying trait of your personality. These people need more than access to make them happy: They need to know that they are being considered not as the category in which to be placed but as people who have many favorable and unfavorable characteristics.

Avoiding the Consultants

It would be naive to believe that the hearts and minds of all the students were dramatically affected by eleven weeks of intensive exposure to issues of access. In many ways—some conscious, some unconscious; some sophisticated, some clumsy—many students avoided dealing with the consultants and with the needs of different sorts of physically disabled clients. At times I found their cynicism profoundly depressing.

The most obvious way in which students avoided the disability issue was by simply avoiding contact with the consultants. During the first week I repeatedly observed the following pattern: Peter makes a comment to a student and she replies by looking at Lucia (an instructor); Peter speaks to the woman again and she replies to Lucia a second time. Of course, such behavior is understandable and it did not continue throughout the quarter. But many students felt real discomfort about their first conversations with the consultants.

Another barrier resulted from a surprising reluctance to rearrange the furniture in the studio to accommodate people in wheelchairs. At first I interpreted this as insensitivity and inexperience, but when it continued throughout the quarter I began to wonder if the tangle of desks and chairs, and piles of

debris on the floor, were not unconscious ways to avoid interaction. In the cluttered, crowded studio with everyone in a rush
all the time, many opportunities were missed. Here are my
notes:

Dan begins to introduce his part of the site. With three people in
wheelchairs attending, it's a little hard for them all to fit into the space
to get a good look. His first client is "Mrs. Winkelstein," an elderly
eccentric with definite ideas about what she wanted. Her apartment
had to have "a lot of room." The consultants are unable to see the
model at this point. Cheryl and Peter move as well as they can, comment on how hard it is to see, but no one takes the initiative. Dan
does lower the top floor to show it to the consultants, but his back is
to one or another of the consultants at every point.

We move on, with much shifting of wheelchairs, to "Lindsay Anderson." After some time, Tom points out that Cheryl may not be able
to see. They then hold up the mirror, so that Cheryl and Steve can
see. Many questions develop about circulation between bedrooms. We
move to the ground floor. Again, Cheryl has to raise herself up to
see.

We move on to Alan. He begins by talking about the top unit.
Cheryl can't see. Steve is blocking the view. Alan finally moves the
top floor down. Just at this point, when Jeff begins talking, Cheryl
tries to come around to the back of the model. She can't get through;
she mutters. I ask her what the problem is. Finally the students become aware of her and move the model, and she repositions herself.

"Not being able to see" was a recurring problem throughout
the quarter, despite the innovative use of mirrors and slide presentations. And most of the students simply could not figure
out how to explain to Jane what they were doing. One group
tried to describe the site by just walking behind Jane and talking. Peter and Ray intervened, asking them to explain it to Jane,
and Ray moved Jane's hand over the plan. Without Peter and
Ray's intervention, I doubt that the students would have made
any attempt to present the information to Jane in a comprehensible way.

Projection was another avoidance technique. Several students explained that their perceptions of the consultants' shyness or fear prevented them from making contact.

We try to approach Peter more to talk to him, but it's been hard to approach him. He seems to be elusive. I saw him several times in Sproul Plaza and I tried to say hello, but he looked the other way. I think it's shyness. Well, in the studio, I think in most of the cases, the initiative comes from us. . . . It seems that the consultants feel a little afraid, too maybe shy to come. When we are discussing things, I see them pass by and look at us, and I can see in their eyes that they want to come and join the group, but they don't know how to go about it, and they're so afraid of disrupting the conversation that's going on.

One student summarized the stalemate: "Somehow we were saying we'll wait for the consultants to make a move, and they were waiting for us to make a move."

Some of the consultants were concerned or confused about their roles. Peter, for example, spoke about feeling uncomfortable approaching students when they were working at their tables. But all three consultants I interviewed commented that they tried to be sensitive to what they saw as the students' anxiety and confusion. Cheryl pinpointed several of the problems:

There's a kind of ambiguity of goals in this class. It's a studio, and students are designing away like mad. They're not looking at themselves as being in a class to learn about disability. And they're not likely to use studio time to ask all the questions they need to ask about disability. After all, they're not expected to probe into the lives of their teachers, or their clients, for that matter, except in certain ways. Some feel that the information would be very interesting but not exactly relevant, so perhaps they have no business asking it. I don't think it's just plain anxiety.

Some students made contact with Cheryl but ignored the other consultants. Cheryl was indeed the most gregarious, open, and approachable of the consultants, and she was present in the studio more hours than any of the others. But Cheryl may also have been the least threatening because her disability is, to an able-bodied person like me, less severe than Jane's blindness, Steve's speech difficulties, or Peter's fragility. (Steve and Peter were both ill at times during the quarter.) Most of the students rarely talked to the other consultants unless they had particular questions. Mary summarized the general style in her journal: "I do feel uncomfortable just talking with the disabled people unless I have something concrete to say, except with Cheryl. I don't mind asking her questions or just her opinion on how things feel to her. I do think she made the effort by just coming over to see what we were up to. She is also very inspirational. She shows her enthusiasm, which at this point is usually all we need to keep us going."

Some design teams became so involved in the traumas of the group process that they avoided all other issues. One group even became "divorced." Given the threat that the disabled consultants appeared to pose to some students, however, it is possible that getting bogged down in interpersonal conflicts was a way of avoiding contact with the consultants. Similarly, some teams allowed themselves to become sidetracked by focusing on the disagreements between consultants and instructors.

Avoiding Disability-Related Issues

The most obvious way to avoid confronting disability issues was to create "normal," well-adjusted, Hollywood-style disabled people as hypothetical clients. The two independent Vietnam veterans, Roy Clearwater and Henry Keaton, are dramatic cases in point. Alan described Roy as a "very friendly person. . . . He knows everyone and he's friends with everyone there, and they like him and he likes them. . . . [He's] a certain center—in terms of warmth or something—in that small residence area." Nancy described Roy as "very congenial" with many friends "who come over to visit him a lot." Henry Keaton, though much less sociable, has three women help him out in various ways. As Alan explains: "He's got this other lady who lives down—god, it's just like a soap opera—who's got the hots for him." Add to these attractive gentlemen one beautiful paraplegic who is forever surrounded by attentive men, and one saintly single parent who sacrifices all for her disabled daughter, and a cast of characters for a second *Coming Home* emerges.

In the final pages of her journal, one perceptive student noted her group's tendency to romanticize the characters they created: "I felt all along that the character we had made Roy out to be was a cop-out. The rest of the group saw him as wanting to play down his handicap, but it's true that the image doesn't mesh with his strong, well-adjusted personality. That's a very important point and I'm sorry I didn't press the issue earlier on when it occurred to me. I guess being outnumbered I shied away."

Some students avoided the issue simply by investing very little in the creation of the characters. Although many of the flat and shallow stereotypes in the early weeks were fleshed out as the quarter progressed, some of the characters remained vague and uninteresting, and the stories told about them were correspondingly drab. When I asked students early on whether their blind characters had been blind since birth, only one of the students had previously considered the question. Other students admitted that they were uncertain about how a wheelchair-bound man managed to get up in the morning or put himself to bed at night; they had not thought about whether he needed an attendant.

Avoidance, of course, was not cut and dried; lively arguments ensued when differing viewpoints clashed. This extract from the last entries in Mac's journal shows his group in conflict:

Our group works like this: First, John decides we've got to do something in order to ace the other groups. For example: We shouldn't be fearful of using ramps for disabled access. Everyone else, including supergroup, are scared about ramps and leaving them till last.

Mac: So we make it an intrinsic part of the design—a ramp that is nonthreatening and nonexclusive—one everyone uses and doesn't feel uncomfortable or conspicuous.

Peter and Hung: Yeah—How?

Mac: Er . . . uh . . . well . . . we design! (A joke)

John: Look how much space a ramp with a twelve-to-one ratio takes up!

Peter: We'll never fit it without it being conspicuous.

John: Really, let's forget it.

Mac: What?! This is the most important part of this assignment! If we forget it because of space—that's really arrogant!

John: If we use elevators, that's access!

Hung: But they break.

John: Ramps are ugly.

Hung and Mac: So let's make ours pretty as well as convincing.

John: (Adopting his devil's-advocate approach): Ramps are ugly. The process leading to ramps is ugly. Why should we bother changing our entire design for—what is it?—ten percent of the population or less even that needs access when the elevator breaks down one percent of the time?

Mac, Peter, Hung: (Stunned silence.)

Peter: I think your attitude needs softening.

Reassessing Preconceptions and Experiences

To my surprise, at least one-third of the students had a close friend or relative who was or had been disabled in some way. Some of them did not realize it themselves until we were well into the quarter, and they commented that they had not thought about it until they took this course. George spoke about a client for whom he had designed a house during the summer. Only now did he begin to understand why she had insisted that the ramp be unobtrusive. He realized that she did not want anyone to know that a disabled person lived there, that she felt ashamed of her disability, which had resulted from a skiing accident.

Lisa recorded in her journal how reading Lifchez and Winslow's *Design for Independent Living* had led her to think again about two disabled students she knew:

What struck me most is the drastic transition people had to make to live "on their own." I guess I'd always thought that they had led similar lives at home—naive, huh? When I lived on the floor in the dorm with Mark and Marie I learned, in talking to them, the difficulties they were facing now, day to day, but neither talked about their childhood all that much, just recent things. I became aware of the problems someone with cerebral palsy might have through Marie— like the times when her attendants didn't show up. One morning Marie had to bang on Chris and Lanny's wall to get her, and the elevator was always a pain—her chair got hung up on the ridges. Marie always explained her past as being on her own. I guess her Mom can't take care of her; Marie says they don't get along anyway— and she's always lived in hospitals and homes.

Several students recalled parents who were disabled in some way. Nathan, for example, wrote about his father:

There are things that come out in my journal that I never thought about, that had nothing to do with the class. I was talking to Cheryl, and somehow we got into drug abuse among handicapped people. We talked about that, and I never realized before that my father was disabled. He's dead now. I never realized before—I never thought of him as disabled. He was injured on the job; he broke his back. I never realized, because I lived with it for so long, that he always had a drug problem. It was really strange to "flash" on, to realize. I looked at my childhood differently. It really kind of hurts, to realize that my father was always drugged out because he was disabled. I guess he was always hurting; going to the doctor. Eventually it killed him.

Dianne's father contracted polio when she was two. Like Nathan, she recorded poignant recollections in her journal. Recalling her "one memory of him walking"—when he carried her upstairs on his shoulders to bed—she reflected:

He's my father. He's in a wheelchair. I never heard the word "disabled." He just couldn't walk—that's all. He is a normal person who happens to get around by using his arms to push his wheelchair rather than using legs to walk.

When I was a child my feelings about his situation were mostly that I was lucky because I got to ride around in his wheelchair. I was given the hope by my mother that someday he might walk and my sister and I were to pray to make it possible. I now resent it that we weren't told it was impossible—it must've been torture for my father to hear our prayers every night.

For Chloe, the experience triggered memories of her grandfather, who was paralyzed on one side at age thirty-five. Like many of the students, she commented that she felt that she should see all disabled people as she saw him: as a normal person:

I grew up with that, seeing that as natural because I never saw him any other way. I never saw him walking normally. He couldn't talk too well. I think it was his right side that was paralyzed; he couldn't write too well. He couldn't control his right foot. I saw my grandfather as a normal person. Every morning he would sit in his bed and use this rail kind of thing so he could stand up without help from anybody.

So every morning I saw him doing that and it was normal. It never struck me. But that was my grandfather. Now when I go out and see somebody who cannot walk or who is blind, I do not see him or her as a normal person. I see him as a disabled person. That's how I see these consultants. And I think it shouldn't be that way. I should see them as I saw my grandfather.

Many students expressed their preconceptions about disability in journal entries. Some identified their biases early and acknowledged the effect they were having on their work. Early in the quarter John said: "I've never really had any contact with a blind person or a person in a wheelchair. It's hard to get past that barrier, hard to get past the fact that I don't want to offend this guy by asking something I shouldn't." And Nathan was quite willing to admit, at the end of the quarter, his preconceptions about Steve: "I've got to admit, the first time I saw him—I saw him before I was in this class—I figured he was really . . . he was probably mentally retarded, just really out of it. But I've just gotten to know him as a person. I've realized . . . just how 'insane' he is. He's really a good example of that, while someone like Cheryl is still fairly straight."

Most of the students were curious about the consultants' disabilities, however reluctant they were to ask questions. Early in the quarter Bill confided: "Pete just looks a bit strange. His body is so, I mean, his head is almost normal size and his body is just so dwarfed. It's a curiosity. I hate to say it like that, but it is." Bill's curiosity was not limited to disability:

I've watched Peter and Steve's female friends with both of them and at first I thought, "Where's her head at? What's her motivation? How's she getting off on this or whatever?" Then the more I observed them together, the more I thought, this is pretty nice. I think it's a bisexual thing, because of a couple of comments, and I thought well, shoot, that's great. Given that whole picture of it, I thought it was just fantastic . . . obviously the two gentlemen are a little bit disadvantaged, but the girls have that and each other so I think that makes up for it. I think that's great. I think it's beautiful.

Steve was perhaps the consultant who occasioned the most nervousness in the beginning and probably won over the most students in the end with his infectious humor. I remember my own acute discomfort the day Steve rode his minimotorcycle into the classroom and then dismounted with great banging and crashing and flailing of arms. The students did not know where to look; I found myself looking at Jane's eyes. Chloe described what she grew to appreciate about Steve: "He swears like a trooper. And he knows that if he reaches out to touch something, he's gonna destroy it probably, but he does it anyway. And I don't mind, because he goes 'Ohh WOW!' and he reaches out and . . . goes 'Oh, I'm sorry.' He's not at all removed. He moves around and gets excited and he jokes around and he talks about everything else but the project, which I get a lot out of." Bill struggled to explain how he felt toward Steve: "At first, I looked at Peter and Steve and I was just curious about what their problems were, what it would be like to be in their place. I've thought about this a lot. My heart goes out to Steve when he's trying to talk. I want to help him; something in me wants to reach in there and help him bring the words out."

In an interview Chloe and I talked about how she felt when she heard Peter's autobiographical tape:

Chloe: I felt a kind of pity. I felt sorry.
Wendy: I think that's a normal reaction, don't you?
Chloe: Yes, but I shouldn't feel that way, because he *is* a person. I tend to see him as somebody *disabled*; we shouldn't look at them as disabled—they are quite capable; they're intelligent. It's just that they cannot walk or . . . that's secondary, you know. But society influences our thinking, and we look on it as a disadvantage. True, they *are* disadvantaged.

Time and again I heard students reminding themselves that they "shouldn't feel that way" and that "he *is* a person." Later in the quarter Lisa admitted that she was still struggling to empathize with the consultants:

I still don't feel that I could put myself in the place of, say, Steve or Cheryl . . . and experience their environment the way they would experience it. And that is what you want to do as a designer. That's what Ray has been saying and I really agree with that. And I think to do that you've got to know more personally about the person, what it feels like to be that way. Everyone can imagine what it is like to be a little kid, because everyone is a kid at one time. But I've never been handicapped, I've never been confined to a wheelchair, so I don't really understand what it is like. I don't know how it is best handled.

Another set of preconceptions about social roles influenced the development of the female characters. Michael, whose team had created the saintly single mother, Sylvia, admitted that his group had difficulty imagining a mother who was not a full-time homemaker:

I think our group has been brought up with very strong familial re-lationships. And so we all asked ourselves, if any of us were handi-capped what would our families do. And I know if I was handicapped, my mom would never trust anybody to take care of me. As long as I couldn't handle myself, unless I moved away and just broke ties, she would always take the responsibility on herself rather than trust-ing me to a stranger, to somebody who was not a very close friend or relative. So, from our own experiences that was the conclusion we came up with, that Sylvia felt responsible as a mother to take on the burden or whatever: responsibility. And also she felt that her duty as a mother, as a protector, that it was her right in fact, as much as she would suffer through it, it was her right to take it upon herself.

Paul, a member of another group, challenged the stereotype in this way: "Suppose she meets a new guy and he becomes her boyfriend. And then she starts working in this real estate office. Or what's going to happen if this guy moves in with her?" Was it fair to Sylvia, Paul wondered, to build the house around her daughter?

Paul also pointed to stereotypes about social class and leisure time: "When we were writing scenarios, everyone wanted a college professor or something—it just blew my mind. There's absolutely no empathy for the working class. They couldn't develop any kind of feeling for someone who worked eight or nine hours a day and came home and ate dinner and watched TV. Like that wasn't a valid existence, and they couldn't have interests other than that—they at least had to listen to classical music."

Feeling Manipulated

The multiplicity and ambiguity of the course's goals and the presence of the observers made some students uncomfortable.

Lisa said: "Things aren't always quite as spelled out as they could be. You tend to get the feeling that you are being observed, which is fine, but at the beginning Ray said that we were not 'guinea pigs,' but you tend to get that feeling all the way through the class by the way it is set up, and people walking around photographing and asking questions all the time."

When I asked Peter about this issue, he acknowledged that it was a problem: "I'm sure the students do feel manipulated. Essentially I don't think they're being manipulated, but the line's unclear." Steve replied, "We are manipulating their grades—but for a greater social endeavor: sensitizing them to disability." This is legitimate, he claimed, because it is necessary to "use every means imaginable" to fight for the rights of disabled people in a "country that does not promote a climate in which disabled people can live."

Working in design teams, students learned how to share tasks, cooperate, and apportion responsibility. But many were troubled by the painful aspects of group work, and they struggled to cope with the interpersonal conflicts and irrational forces that teamwork can generate.

11

Group Cohesion and Openness to New Experience

Dorsh DeVoe

At the time of the project, Dorsh DeVoe was a graduate student in the Department of Social Welfare at U.C. Berkeley. After completing her doctorate, she worked with refugees in South Asia. She is now associated with a child protection agency in the San Francisco Bay area. This chapter focuses on what proved to be the most difficult task for our students: working in design teams.

Students in this project were taught in groups of four and five. The instructors thought this format would give students a peer group setting—a position of comfort and strength—in which to confront and examine the issue of disability and, more important, interact with the consultants. An analysis of the evaluative measures administered at the end of the first two quarters of the project (the winter and spring quarters of 1979) indicated a clear relationship between a design team's style of functioning as a group and its ability to accommodate the consultants.

The end-of-quarter evaluation gave students a chance to express their feelings about the design and structure of the course, especially the teamwork component, the role of the instructors, and the role of the design consultants. A short questionnaire contained multiple-choice questions about group process, the team members' relationships with one another, and the quality of instruction. (Two open-ended questions were included, but these did not tend to elicit useful answers—perhaps because of time pressure or students' lack of writing experience.) We administered the questionnaire at the beginning of the last class meeting, told the students that the form would take about twenty minutes to fill out, and asked them to put their names at the top of the form, so that we could compare the perceptions of members of each team. Students were quite willing to participate, even though the survey was not anonymous and the questions were quite personal.

We were surprised by the strong response: Within the next few days several staff members were approached by students who wanted to share lengthy stories about how their group worked, the troubles they had with other group members, and the difficulties and joys of designing with team members. Though some students voiced concerns about their relationship to the disabled consultants or the instructors, their talk centered on their group, their feelings about each other, their doubts about the quality of their final models. The sincerity and intensity of these comments suggested that it might be useful to administer a similar set of questions early in the course if only to indicate to the students that, from the start, the staff realized that the group process might be frightening, upsetting, and difficult in ways that students had not experienced when working alone on projects. Making students aware of the process at the outset might help them make more conscientious efforts to nurture their teams' group process and perhaps free them for more creative and exploratory teamwork.

Cohesive and Factious Teams: Winter 1979

To see how students felt about their own team and other teams in the class, we asked each student to name which two people in the class he should most like to work with if they were to do a six-month design project in the near future. Of the twelve teams in the winter 1979 class, seven could be labeled cohesive and five factious based on the following observations: When asked who they would like to work with in the future, members of seven of the teams named, almost exclusively, two people from their own team or—without exception—someone from another of these same seven teams. Thus, these students not only felt confident about their own teams' quality of work but also noticed members of these other cohesive teams. All these students wrote comments that were directed inward, toward themselves and their teams, and they tended to rank their team members quite high on our scales of creativity, talent as designers, flexibility, energy level, ability to facilitate productive work, ability to relate to disabled consultants, and knowledge about disability. Students in these teams gave all their team members high credit for their work, their contributions, and their personal attributes, with no sign that they felt personally threatened by or competitive with the members of their team, at least not in any way they could not handle as a group.

This cluster of teams felt that they worked as a group, and they described the group process as enjoyable and a profitable learning experience. Some of these teams had leaders, others did not, but all felt their style was appropriate and acceptable, that they were at the top of the class in both team effort and final product. The majority of students in these teams felt that their instructors encouraged them to work as a group, that the instructors' interest was genuine and their criticism and suggestions very helpful in the evolution of the final design product. These students also appreciated how the instructors served as a liaison with the design consultants, and many mentioned that they viewed Ray Lifchez's way of talking to the consultants as a model for their own exchanges. Finally, virtually all these students left the course feeling very comfortable relating to the consultants and convinced that the experience would always be useful to them.

In contrast, members of the other five teams expressed a variety of mixed feelings about all aspects of their own teams' process. On the scales for creativity, flexibility, talent as a designer, facilitating, ability to relate to consultants, and knowledge about disability, these students tended to describe themselves and their team members as mediocre.

These students typically believed that their own teams had done less work than others in the class, and they tended to select midrange answers to questions about how well their teams worked as a group, whether they enjoyed working as a group, and whether they needed a leader and did not have one or did not need a leader and had one.

Among team members there was little consensus about how well they worked with the consultants, and most seemed somewhat disappointed at the instructors' effectiveness in the group process and in helping the students relate to the consultants. Many of these students expressed frustration at not knowing what to do with the consultants or how to "meet" them. Perhaps they were somewhat anxious that they were not taking advantage of the course's opportunities.

Various students in the factious groups rated their involvement with the instructors as irregular. They felt that the instructors encouraged them to work as a group only part of the time, and that the instructors and consultants did not seem to relate well to each other.

Thus according to the students themselves, there were successful and unsuccessful teams. From their comments, several recommendations can be extrapolated. First, students want consistency in involvement on the part of all the supporting staff. Instructors must be available for advice and opinions, and they must be seen in the studios with the disabled consultants. Students also need an introduction to the consultants very early in the course. Many of the students pointed to a meeting between the consultants and students held near the end of the quarter as critical in their feelings about the consultants as people as well as about their role in the class. Since the students felt that much of their time and energy with the consultants was spent being afraid of offending them or figuring out ways to meet them, some sort of "icebreaker" exercises might be done in that first meeting. And the instructors must visibly support the role of the consultants in the class, perhaps by always bringing a consultant over whenever he or she approaches a team on some design matter.

Second, the instructor needs to validate the group process itself. The dramatic split between teams that felt strongly the encouragement and support of the staff and those that did not suggests that the instructors themselves may not have been totally supportive of the group process, or that they did not know how to encourage it.

Finally, if from the outset the particular qualities of group work and the roles of the staff in it are articulated, students might be able to be more open with one another in matters that affect the group process and product, much more willing to work through problems with the help of the staff, and more committed to their teams as collaborative entities.

Competition versus Collaboration: Spring 1979

This quarter several issues about the methodology of the course were explained to the students at the start: The physically disabled consultants were introduced and their roles described; the observers and their research intentions were identified; and the fact that the students would work in groups, as design teams, was clearly stated.

Perhaps because group process was introduced at the beginning of the quarter, students' responses to working in teams were more complex than in the preceding quarter. When asked at the end of the course who they would choose to work with in the future, students gave mixed responses, often choosing one person from their original group and another from without, or often leaving the questionnaire item blank. Their answers did not seem to reflect group tensions, personality problems, or group process; nor did students express a feeling that group problems would be resolved or precluded by changing their teams' membership—the simplistic solution often suggested last quarter. While students acknowledged the import of personality dynamics within the teams, they seemed to accept personality as a variable to work with and work through. Competition among the teams ran high. Some students questioned how the team process could be reconciled with the grading of individuals; others wondered how to escape individual competition for grades in order to collaborate with teammates. Several also felt that the team process was too time-consuming, that it robbed individuals of the time and energy they needed to do their personal best. Finally, while students recognized that groups had a greater potential for work than individuals alone, they struggled to decide whether groups needed leadership to channel their energy.

On this issue the teams split into four camps: teams that felt they needed a leader, chose one, and worked well together; teams that felt they did not need leaders, did not identify themselves as having one, and worked well together; teams in which some students did not feel they needed a leader, yet had one, and felt it did not work well; and teams that wanted a leader, yet did not have one, and felt it did not work out well. None of the evidence suggested that leadership was critical to a team's success. Some leaderless teams lamented that a leader would have helped them identify their objectives, work goals, and technical task schedule. But other leaderless groups expressed strong needs for a nonhierarchical democratic process and feared that a leader might have turned into a dictator. One thesis of the course—that leadership must evolve in ways that allow each person to be both leader and follower, rather than being arbitrarily fixed—perhaps needed to be made more explicit to students.

Favoritism was also an issue in this class. Several students worried that their groups' progress was hampered because instructors did not give them equal attention. These students felt that the greater their interaction with the instructors, the better their chances for a higher grade. One student felt that her team had been stigmatized as a loser once it fell behind the other teams. But another student complained that her team was ignored because it appeared to be ahead. Yet another student cited a third criterion: "Many times the staff latches onto the team that best expresses their own ideas and works closely with them, almost as another group member."

This uneven guidance affected the morale of students throughout the quarter. Students who benefited from a spontaneous field trip to a gay area of San Francisco or a dinner with one of the consultants were excited and enthusiastic. But students who felt ignored became alienated, beset by the gnawing questioning of what their group was doing "wrong." While most students appreciated the diversity of the instructors ("The instructors are another group as diverse as any of ours"), a number were frustrated by conflicting opinions or messages from the various staff. Some skepticism over any lecture presentations that offered "slick designs" was expressed by students who thought slickness antithetical to social considerations.

Students' disappointment in instructors is likely to be a measure of their expectations. Once an instructor takes an interest in a group, that group feels it, and neighboring groups see it too. Several groups were waiting to be discovered, and felt they never were. Students seemed to expect a continual dialogue with the instructors, although each was assigned to work with several groups.

Students and Consultants

Students' feelings about the value of having physically disabled people serve as design consultants were quite mixed, though most appreciated the intention of their presence. Several students wished they had seen the consultants more often during the first half of the quarter, when major design decisions were made for the projects. But the consultants felt that students did not seem very interested in drawing them into their designs. Peter told me that, with one exception, students never directly asked him questions, but he had to solicit them himself. He also hypothesized that if it were left to the students to make appointments with the disabled consultants, they would not do so. While Jane said she had hardly ever "connected" with the students, never had a team's total attention during the quarter, and Simon said that he did not feel involved in any team's process, Steve was virtually drawn in as a member of one group, which needed him as a catalyst for decision making.

However uninvolved in the process, the consultants were drawn into the lives of some of the students. In turn, these students' greatest satisfaction with the consultants seemed to be having become personally close to one of them in a chance meeting, at an arranged dinner, or over coffee after class. Several consultants said that their satisfaction with their role came from feeling needed and known, and students also felt that becoming friends was a sign that they were learning about disability and using the consultants well. Thus for both students and consultants companionship, comfortableness, and friendship were more important than accessibility issues per se.

This desire for camaraderie does raise a nagging question: If the consultants' presence was not primarily to raise issues of accessibility, then what is the course about—disability? If their presence is primarily to present students with an opportunity to be friends with people who look different and have different problems, then why are they called "design consultants" and not just clients or users? Students assume that design consultants will have something instructive to teach them as architects, yet consultants were waiting for students to relate to them "beyond" their disabilities and did not want to be considered as experts for their handicaps. If the role of the disabled consultants is not to be entirely focused on disability, then are they simply to act as advisors and lay users? Too, students need facts and specific information about disability before they can appreciate that access is not the sole concern of disabled users.

Finally, several students noted a tension between the instructors and consultants, and they said they rarely saw instructors working with the consultants in the studio. One student asked me in irritation if it was "acceptable" for disabled people to be late, if they were entitled to special allowances that slowed down the class. Other students commented that if the consultants were to serve as surrogate instructors, then they should be chosen for their ability and willingness to talk about disability and the built environment. Some wished that the range of disabilities represented by the various consultants had been broader, more representative of the range of disabilities in society at large.

In an advanced summer class, students teamed up with design consultants to provide services to local groups, such as this community task force that was planning for a senior center in Oakland. The clients' eagerness to meet federal and state guidelines for accessibility provided a powerful source of validation for the consultants' role.

12

A Richer Mix

Fran Katsuranis

During the summer session of 1979 an advanced studio course was offered at U.C. Berkeley. Unlike the introductory course, this class gave students the opportunity to work with real clients on actual community projects. Fran Katsuranis, then a doctoral student in the Sociology Program at the University of California at San Francisco, served as an outside observer. She is now working as a consultant for the State of California, Child Health and Disability Prevention Program.

The summer class of nineteen students—fourteen men and five women—included graduate, recently graduated, and advanced undergraduate students of varied architectural experience. Several students had been or were employed in architectural firms either part- or full-time; most of the undergraduates were in their final year of studies and had completed an earlier studio class. Thus for many students this course served as a transition: For some it was the final course before seeking employment; for others it was a stepping stone from employment into graduate school.

The studio met four days a week, three hours a day, for eight weeks. Four physically disabled design consultants worked with the students, typically rotating among the groups and providing consultation as requested or appropriate. One of the consultants had recently completed her graduate studies in architecture at Berkeley; the other three had worked with earlier studio classes.

The students divided themselves into four design teams, each with a different design problem and client group:

Northgate: the renovation of a historic building on the Berkeley campus in order to make it accessible to physically disabled users.

Orinda Church Housing: the development of housing for the elderly on a site owned by a church in the nearby town of Orinda.

Friendship House: the planning of housing and workshop facilities for a group of individuals, both able-bodied and physically disabled, who lived and worked as an extended family in Berkeley.

Sojourner Truth Manor: the program and design of a community center to be built as an extension to housing for the elderly in a black neighborhood in Oakland.

The initial agreements with the clients were handled by Ray Lifchez; projects were solicited, expectations clarified, and terms negotiated before the summer session began. Each of these design problems was an actual project that would conceivably be undertaken by the clients. Each client group included a sampling of potential users, planners, financers, and other concerned parties. One or more individuals from each group were available to the students on a regular basis.

Selecting and Accepting the Project

Virtually all the students identified the direct participation of clients and the feasibility of the projects as what they liked best about the course. They regarded the studio as not just another class but as an opportunity to function as professionals in a real situation. It seemed important to them to be able to take their projects seriously and to be taken seriously, and they appeared to give considerable thought to their selection of the project they would work on.

Particularly important in the selection process was a student's impression of the "reality" of the project: its feasibility, the likelihood of its being carried out, and the clients' commitment and enthusiasm. One student mentioned, for example, that one reason he did not choose the Friendship House project was that the client's choice of site did not lend itself to the construction required, and he wanted to work on a project that seemed more likely to be realized.

An equally important factor in the selection of a project was the challenge it represented—the opportunity to tackle some new issue. For some students the primary challenge was a particular design requirement: the topography of the site, the inaccessibility of a building, economic factors, or the meeting of guidelines imposed by the Department of Housing and Urban Development (HUD). Other students looked to the social worthiness of the project as most critical. A third source of challenge was the particular client group. Students also took into account which of their peers they wanted to work with.

The issue of establishing and maintaining professional credibility proved to be a major theme throughout the course, appearing in various forms in the students' relationships with clients, peers, consultants, and instructors. Students selected their projects with a view to demonstrating and perfecting their architectural skills, and they looked for clients who could provide this opportunity. For the most part they assessed the clients in terms of their enthusiasm and commitment to the project. As it turned out, the clients who were most willing to relate to the students as professionals were those at the Sojourner Truth Manor. These black seniors were the least knowledgeable about architecture but the most enthusiastic and cooperative of the client groups. In contrast, students found the journalism faculty members who acted as clients for the Northgate project difficult to track down; they did not appear to take the project, or the students, seriously. These faculty-clients tended to treat the student-designers as students. For example, during their first meeting these clients quizzed the students about their knowledge of a media center. The students, who had expected to take charge of the interview, were surprised, embarrassed, and immediately put on the defensive.

The Friendship House project posed the opposite problem. Although Peter Trier, as spokesperson for the clients, was readily available to the students and enthusiastic about the project, it became apparent that he expected from the students a more personal and intense involvement than they considered professionally appropriate. He related to the students personally, as potential friends or converts to his beliefs, rather than as professionals. Students found his behavior confusing and threatening, both personally and professionally. The three students who selected this project, and those who did not, were also influenced by what they viewed as the formidable challenge of working with Peter, whom they viewed as severely disabled. This challenge they defined in personal and interpersonal, rather than only professional, terms; as one student stated in explaining why he did not choose that project: "I want to enjoy my summer."

Others, including some students who ultimately chose to work on other projects, viewed the possibility of working with Peter as an intriguing opportunity to resolve some of their fears and ignorance about physical disability and the disabled. One student mentioned that he chose the Friendship House project only after he became aware that another student who had signed up for it shared his strong feelings of aversion. At first he had thought he was alone in his feelings, but then decided that "if he can do it, I can too."

Establishing Relationships with Clients

Each group reported having difficulties in scheduling their time. Class time was never considered sufficient for working as a design group and meeting with clients, and most students regularly worked many hours on the project outside of class. Students also kept an informal (and sometimes formal) tally on how many hours they saw other groups working, and who worked evenings and weekends. In large part, time in the studio was equated with commitment to the project, and thus to the team; work outside the studio did not seem to count, or at least not as heavily. Thus students who spent less time in the studio were viewed with suspicion, their commitment questioned. But students who put in considerably more time than others were also suspect.

Scheduling meetings with clients presented problems of coordination. Most of the clients had other demands on their time, and, as could be expected, their ordering of priorities and commitment to the project differed from the students'. As suggested by the instructors, meetings were split between the design studio and the client's home base. Students thus had the opportunity to host and be hosted, and this exchange allowed both students and clients to experience firsthand something of one another's worlds. The exchange also served to equalize the relationship, as each party had the chance to serve as expert in its own setting. This opportunity was particularly valuable in the Sojourner Truth Manor project, perhaps since the differences between clients and students in terms of age, race, and background were the most marked; there was so much to be learned from one another.

The meetings typically involved several client representatives and several students. Managing this complex situation was difficult, particularly when either or both parties were large, diverse in their viewpoints, or disorganized. Several students found it frustrating to try to elicit clear information from clients during group interviews. One complained that the flow of the interview was erratic and difficult to follow; another observed that each member of the client group seemed to have his or her own opinions and concerns, which left the students with a set of conflicting demands.

Initially, Lifchez and some of the instructors served as facilitators to assist the students and clients in coming together. Lifchez laid the ground rules for scheduling meetings, and he and the other instructors offered suggestions to the students about the kinds of questions to ask clients, how to present information to them, and the like. But, of course, any facilitator is both liaison and middleman; that is, in bringing the two sides together the facilitator also stands between them. Thus although the initial contact and agreements were negotiated by Lifchez rather than the students, once the teams began to work the clients were to regard the students as in charge. To encourage the clients to do so, the instructors attended only some of the meetings between students and clients and served as observers rather than participants. In this way the instructors were able to provide guidance and support to students as needed without compromising their independence. The clients' active engagement in the project, however, at times required the instructors' participation, which the clients interpreted as a measure of the projects' credibility. Occasionally instructors intervened on the students' behalf to elicit the clients' continued cooperation, validate a design, or underscore a point.

A confusion of the lines of authority and accountability hampered at least one design team, whose members rejected the terms of participation that its client had negotiated with Lifchez. This disagreement over the nature and degree of involvement of the designers with the client group caused some confusion and resentment between the students and the clients. Each side felt that the other's expectations for the working relationship were unreasonable and unacceptable.

Working as a Team

Students quickly realized that learning about their teammates' architectural preferences, professional experience and ability, interpersonal skills, and cultural reference points was an important prerequisite for establishing an effective design team. But students approached this task with varying degrees of enthusiasm and skill. For the smallest group, a team of three working on the Friendship House project, there seemed little question that all would work together on a single design. These students shared a serious commitment to the project and spent long hours working together, in the process coming to know one another's skills, limitations, and quirks quite well.

The larger teams, those with five or six members, seemed to have more options for organizing their labor and more leeway in the intensity of involvement required of each member. In one group two members who were living together chose to work together at home; their four teammates followed the pattern and paired up. In another group, two students who had worked together effectively in the past assumed the unofficial role (later validated by the group) of chief designers; other group members organized around them.

Ethnic or cultural diversity was mentioned by some students as posing as a barrier to working together. Interestingly, the majority of foreign students clustered in one team. Although this team's members were the ones who raised the issue of cultural barriers, they also formed one of the most tightly knit and effective design groups. Perhaps the very conspicuousness of their diverse backgrounds and perspectives encouraged them to address their differences openly and directly. These students reported that many compromises were made on behalf of the group, but the compromises were not a point of regret or resentment.

The major difficulty in every team's operation was organization: defining the tasks, assigning individual responsibility, determining schedules, and setting deadlines. The central issue faced by each team was to discover a leader and then permit that person to help the team take charge of organizing its efforts. In interviews at the end of the course, most students described their colleagues in the architecture program at large as aggressive and competitive, almost cutthroat, intent on getting top grades and unwilling to share ideas for fear of losing a competitive advantage. Although in the studio there appeared to be a norm of peer acceptance, this acceptance seemed motivated, at least initially, not by mutual trust but by the desire to guard against any one person getting the upper hand. At the beginning of the class, team members seemed reluctant to designate or accept one individual in a leadership role; and individual students, unwilling to shoulder responsibility for the whole group, were hesitant to take an assertive role. In at least one instance a student who did assume a rather aggressive role, expressing his ideas and opinions rather frequently and at great length, was ostracized by his team members.

When later asked what would have helped them to organize themselves better, many students wished that the instructors had appointed team leaders on a rotating basis, or more actively helped them to determine tasks, responsibilities, and deadlines. They found the requirement that each group write out a detailed schedule of tasks and responsibilities very useful in helping them to organize their work and in assuring the accountability of individual group members. The students, in other words, were eager to cede the balance of power to acknowledged legitimate authority rather than negotiate among themselves an alternative egalitarian arrangement.

Lack of experience—in working in a group, in using design consultants, and in tackling a complicated design problem on a short schedule—also impeded progress. The more experienced students faced a dilemma: To the extent that they attempted to capitalize on their expertise, they were open to criticism from team members who viewed this as a threat to the tenuous balance of peer power; but because they were aware of the need for organization and knew ways to achieve it, their frustration with the group's disorganization was acute.

Ultimately, each group did achieve—sometimes by default—some form of organization. As mentioned, one group worked as a set of two-person teams, each with its own design. A second group somewhat reluctantly designated one outspoken graduate student as chief administrator; two members who had worked together previously were labeled chief and assistant designer; the other two members (who were either less assertive or less available) were assigned responsibility for constructing the model and drawing up detailed plans and graphics.

The two other groups devised somewhat more egalitarian structures. In one group of five, an older and experienced student was gradually encouraged, even pushed, to assume a leadership role. Although she was initially reluctant to do so, her frustration with the group's inefficient functioning forced her to assume major responsibility in helping her team get organized. She encouraged her teammates to discuss openly the problems they were experiencing in working together, and they recognized and respected her leadership skills. Once organized, team members all felt more or less equally a part of the final design.

The small three-member team also had some difficulties in achieving an equitable distribution of labor and responsibility. Two of the members were older and more assertive, and they were afraid of intimidating their younger partner, who was more experienced in design but a slow, painstaking worker. All three made a conscious effort to maintain equal participation in design decisions and responsibility, and they were intent on developing a team design. Gradually the group worked out the compromises and understandings necessary to achieve some equilibrium in the team effort. The slower student learned to work faster and to settle for less than perfection, and the other two learned that he did not expect them to match him hour for hour in the studio. Team unity was facilitated in part by the common difficulty they experienced in working with their client.

Clarifying Expectations and Requirements

Typically, architects are presented with a set of design requirements and expected to translate these into an architectural plan. The clients' requirements may be more or less explicit or flexible; may stem from economic, topographical, ideological, or aesthetic concerns; and may be many or few, feasible or impractical, congruent or conflicting. In this class, however, students had to deal with the expectations and requirements of several constituencies: their instructors, the design consultants, and the designated clients.

A number of students mentioned that since the projects were designed in the context of a class and Raymond Lifchez was the primary instructor, he was actually the primary client. As one student expressed it, "The client is the one who pays. Ray is the chief client—he pays with grades." In addition to Lifchez, three other architects served as instructor-consultants, each assigned to one design group. Though the exact role and authority of these instructors remained unclear, students respected their expertise and considered their suggestions seriously; the instructors' requirements were also, they felt, to be incorporated into the design. Similarly, the physically disabled design consultants, who rotated to work with all the groups, formed a second constituency whose suggestions were solicited and whose expectations were regarded seriously.

Of course, students also addressed themselves to the clients for whom the design was to be developed and who, in most cases, were the intended users of the completed project. Although the students worked to help their clients clarify their needs and expectations, some clients seemed to have had a hidden agenda that became apparent only as the quarter proceeded. Thus while the students sought to elicit information, draw up a program, and develop a creative design scheme, several clients seemed to define their project, its goals and success, in other terms. For example, one student suspected that his clients were less interested in developing a good design than in having a set of architectural plans drawn (free of charge) that could be used to raise money to fund the buildings' renovation. The client for Friendship House was suspected of being more concerned with developing a personal relationship with the students, or possibly recruiting them as members of his church, than with the design scheme. Observations of client-student interactions tended to support such suspicions. Certainly, it is not unusual for clients to have multiple agendas, but the upshot for the students was that some clients judged their work in terms quite different from those the students anticipated or could control. These mismatched expectations occasionally led to mutual, though mild, disappointment or frustration, with each party feeling let down in some way.

From their clients the students wanted visions; instead they often got lightbulbs, as their clients were initially concerned with the most practical of requirements, the location of light fixtures and stairs, rather than the creative potential of the building. The disparity in perspectives seemed to be an issue for all the groups to some degree, although at least one design team felt that by the end of the session the two perspectives had produced a healthy synergy.

In the Northgate project, one of the journalism faculty representing the client group had architectural training and had developed an elaborate program of requirements that specified the square footage of rooms, office assignments, and the like. The students felt inhibited by the detail and blocked in their efforts to alter the design. Their client had overwhelmed them with specifics but offered no conceptual basis for a design solution. For example, they sensed that political considerations motivated certain design choices (office size and location); but since these were not explicated, the students were unable to design a suitable alternative.

The distinction between conceptual and specific requirements was also underscored in the students' evaluation of their instructors. Again, the conceptual critique was viewed as more helpful than the criticism or rejection of a specific aspect of the design or the presentation. As one student explained, when the instructor gave conceptual suggestions "the student could alter them to fit his or her own design. This is the most rewarding way of designing."

Gathering Information

Since most of the students had not worked directly with clients, they needed to learn what kinds of information clients could provide, how best to elicit it, and how to translate this information into a design. Here the instructors and consultants played a significant role, helping students to formulate questions for clients and advising them on how to organize the interviews.

Additionally, at least some of the clients and design consultants spent time with the students outside of class, over meals and on field trips. Almost without exception, the students mentioned these experiences as having exerted considerable influence on their perceptions and insights. Students in one group, for example, visited their project site with the design consultants in order to see the building through the eyes of physically disabled users. They photographed a young man with cerebral palsy attempting to climb the many stairs of the building on his knees; they watched while a woman blind from birth demonstrated the danger of an unrailed ledge to the unsuspecting individual with limited vision. Afterward at a local restaurant, they again watched the young man crawl up a flight of wooden stairs to gain access; they helped him to feed himself and marveled as he struggled to extract his wallet from his daypack. The students recounted this experience, and others of the same order, in detail and with emotion. The field visits, they felt, helped them both to understand their clients' design requirements and to view the physically disabled as individuals with valid needs.

The question of how much time and what type of experiences are necessary or useful to facilitate the client-designer relationship was raised as an issue by the team working on the Friendship House project. Here the clients were eager for an intimacy that the students thought unprofessional and inappropriate. In part, the conflict seemed to reflect the students' disapproval of and discomfort with the clients' lifestyle; they did not want to acquire firsthand experience. The question of whether, or to what degree, their lack of direct experience and information detracted from their final design remained unresolved at the end of the course. The clients maintained there was a deficiency.

Resolving Conflicts

Conflicts between instructors, or between student and instructor, seemed the most difficult—or unsettling—for the students. For the most part, students regarded their instructors as experts and were inclined to accept their suggestions as valid. The instructors' comments for or against a particular architectural style were frequently viewed by students not only as a personal reference but also as a requirement they would have to respect, at least if they valued a good grade. (Although students decried the general obsession with and competition for grades, they seemed never to lose sight of their significance.) The instructors, however much they chose to downplay it, exerted considerable influence over the students' perceptions of their own and others' work.

Expertise weighed heavily in the resolution of conflicts, especially conflicts of opinion between the students and their clients. The students tried to affirm their architectural expertise by educating clients to their perspective. They assisted the clients in interpreting the graphic presentations, using the working models, and explicating their needs. But on some issues the clients and the design consultants were clearly in a position to educate the students. If a design consultant objected that a bathroom was too small for a wheelchair, for example, the comment received little argument from the students. But if the same consultant were to critique the design on aesthetic terms, a debate over expertise was more likely to arise. Without exception, the students viewed the design consultants as outsiders, though knowledgeable outsiders, to architecture. Although students valued the design consultants' insights on issues of access and disability, they gave far less credence to the consultants' general opinions about design; students accepted the imposition of practical constraints but spoke disparagingly of the lack of architectural vision that they implied.

On issues related to costs, clearly the clients were in a position to dictate to the students. For the Friendship House project, the students considered the site selected by the client to be too small and recommended another site. To strengthen their argument, they developed two designs, one for the client's site, the other on the second lot which they preferred. Despite the spatial advantages of the larger site, however, the lower purchase price of the smaller property favored the client's original preference.

Implications for the Project

This summer session was a bonus for the project Architectural Design with the Physically Disabled User in Mind; at the outset the project's plan did not anticipate the participation of real-life clients. A studio course that affords such participation seems the obvious next step in the professional curriculum, allowing architecture students to progress to the ever-increasing complexities of professional work. Compared to the basic studio course, in which students created imaginary clients, in this advanced class the design consultants had a stronger role in the design process. First, the students appreciated the consultants' expert knowledge as useful in expediting the clients' projects; second, the clients looked upon the consultants as serious and useful adjuncts to the design process. Thus the consultants' role was validated to the students by not only their instructors but also their clients. Learning about access from physically disabled people also armed students with a new expertise that seemed to elevate their confidence in their interactions with clients.

The design consultants reported mixed feelings when they contrasted the experiences of working with imaginary scenarios and real clients. On the one hand, the consultants felt the presence of clients presented a more lifelike and therefore more interesting situation in which to work. But on the other, the consultants complained that in situations when students could not skillfully judge how to integrate clients' needs and access requirements, the students sometimes paid more attention to what the clients said than to what the consultants said. From my interviews with the design consultants throughout this project, I surmise that they felt somewhat piqued at being upstaged by the clients, whom the students identified as the authority figures.

The clients were fully appreciative of the participation of the physically disabled consultants. All four projects by law had to meet accessibility standards, and the clients were relieved to find that their projects would be conceptualized from the ground up with access in mind.

We came to realize that client accommodation is not merely the third element in design, alongside aesthetics and technology, but is in fact the context within which all factors of architectural design must be placed.

Conclusion

Up until World War II most buildings in the United States were designed without the assistance of architects. Architects were commissioned by wealthy citizens and powerful institutions to design "important" buildings: imposing commercial structures, grand residences, churches, state capitols, museums, and the like. Such buildings are the ones we have come to admire as culturally significant monuments, as works of art, and as symbols of society's achievements and values. These buildings also form the core examples, the masterworks, used to instruct students in architectural design and history.

Ideally, the academic study of the architectural masterwork includes the client-patron's story, for therein lies a partial explanation of the building. Yet we rarely hear about the ordinary people who were to use these buildings, the client-users. This lacuna in our historical understanding is regrettable and yet, in a certain way, not surprising. The architect employed by the munificent client-patron assumed that the client-users' aspirations matched those of their benefactors. Concern for ordinary people and their lives was not perceived as an issue, and the client-users' particular needs were of little or no importance in the vast scheme of things.

Today there are surely far more client-patrons than ever, but the traditional paternalistic concept of patronage has faded. After World War II, architecture "went public," so to speak, and a multiplying legion of architects began to offer a vast array of services to a diverse cast of client groups: neighborhoods, civic committees, government agencies, and public and private corporations. With this change in professional opportunities, architects began to realize that the traditional assumptions about client-users were no longer tenable, a realization that informs current architectural practice and education.

To understand these changes, we can look to the lessons of urban renewal in the United States, a movement conceived in the late 1940s to eradicate urban slums and provide new housing and commercial districts. Under the banner of civic progress, the states and the federal government enacted complex packages of legislation that established a statutory framework, an administrative system, and public financing for urban renewal projects.[1] During the 1950s the revival and enhancement of selected parts of targeted cities was achieved, but often at the expense of the urban poor and minorities, who were displaced when residential blocks were converted to commercial uses and when expensive new housing replaced affordable older units. As cities fulfilled their desire to create new kinds of civic "monuments," numberless people were shunted about, and historic architecture was laid to waste.

It was only after a critical mass of lay and professional people began to make their protests heard in the mid-sixties that the dislocating effects of urban renewal were seriously debated and the destruction slowly came to a halt. But from its inception and for some twenty-five years, 1950 to 1975, urban renewal in its various programmatic forms did more to raise public awareness about the social and political nature of the urban environment than had any issue in our nation's history. Concepts and programs for urban rehabilitation spawned by urban

1. See James Q. Wilson, ed., *Urban Renewal: The Record and the Controversy* (Cambridge: MIT Press, 1966), 129–38.

renewal provided architects with heretofore unknown opportunities to build, and also brought social scientists, in the vanguard of those who fought urban renewal, into a public arena with architects. Because architects had been given enormous opportunities by urban renewal, they were often unfavorably identified with its negative effects. For example, student strikes at Columbia University in the spring of 1968 were sparked by protests over the effects that proposed urban renewal projects would have on neighborhoods near the Morningside Heights campus. Students of architecture were among the most outspoken and the first to sit in.

The architecture profession was genuinely embarrassed by the attention and, in some cases, by its members' involvement in urban renewal projects that had been heralded as socially beneficent but which turned out quite otherwise. During this same period the profession was affected by the civil rights movement, which compelled a new recognition of ethnicity that included the rights of communities to express themselves through their architecture, and by the demands of physically disabled Americans for a more accessible environment and equal opportunities in employment, education, housing, and transportation.

It became clear that to design well for client-users, practitioners would need training and skills beyond those provided by the traditional curriculum in architecture, engineering, and architectural history. Architects recognized that social scientists had a certain kind of knowledge that pertained to design, particularly to the design of large-scale works whose client-users were members of diverse social and ethnic groups. Architects sensibly admitted that not all questions about the relationships between people and buildings could be addressed through plain common sense and humaneness.

Thus social scientists, mainly sociologists and psychologists, were invited to take part in architectural practice, and in the late 1960s and early 1970s schools of architecture began to bring them aboard. The profession's invitation to social scientists implied the tacit recognition that client-users could not be taken for granted, could not be typed in the image of either the architect or the client-patron. The profession now needed a new paradigm for the architect-client relationship—a most significant change.

And so in architecture schools social scientists began offering classes based on their own disciplines, courses that drew students' attention to both larger and more subtle issues of design in which human accommodation was paramount. Interested students began to explore new interdisciplinary approaches that combined architecture and the social sciences, and some schools devised doctoral programs for a new kind of architectural practitioner, one who conducted research in the social basis of design. Studio courses also incorporated the influence of social scientists' thinking.

Unquestionably, social scientists have contributed to the humanizing of our concept of architectural design. But we might ask whether some of their message is lost when *social factors* per se are introduced in the design studio. For architecture students tend to express a certain disquiet at the mention of "pure" social science concepts, sociological and psychological materials that have not been "translated" into design factors. Indeed, if students are to develop a coherent conceptual framework, it seems that social factors must be transformed into design concepts, since otherwise students tend to fear that social science might straitjacket their architectural creativity. This dangerous misconception about client accommodation as antithetical to creative expression can be dispelled only by teaching students how to be client-conscious and make beautiful buildings at the same time.

Our project was by no means the first pedagogical effort to integrate the subjects of people and buildings. By sensitively presenting the issue of ethnicity and culture, for example, community-oriented architects have been teaching studio classes of predominantly middle-class students how to successfully design buildings for client groups unlike themselves. But we found only a little of this experience to be of much use when we began to implement our project, largely because we did not want to present physically disabled people as a *special* population for whom one could design *special* environments. Before we could raise any design issues we had to help students and design consultants see themselves in one another: Our students needed to discover the human connection between themselves and disabled people, and our design consultants needed to discover how to participate effectively in the design process. Through our focus on disability we hoped to heighten students' sensitivity to human frailty and vulnerability, which were to be understood as the inevitable complements to vigor and strength in the human life cycle.

Though our formal project has ended, at Berkeley we continue to work with physically disabled consultants in our studio classes as we search for new ways to improve students' abilities to learn and ours to teach. We have come to realize that client accommodation is not merely the third element in design, alongside aesthetics and technology, but is in fact the context within which all factors of architectural design must be placed: "Rather than any kind of analytical, 'objective,' or abstract approach, the architect-teacher is usually able to place before students a more holistic, experience-based, insightful perspective on the making of habitable places. . . . In this sense, we are not talking about 'user-oriented design,' the way one might talk about structures, energy efficiency, or style, but rather about all these ingredients as they relate to people's lives."[2]

But individual courses and individual teachers are, in professional education, only as effective as their school when it comes to making a profound change in how preprofessional students think, how they will practice, and whether they will receive professional support in practicing what they have been taught. Any one architectural design course, for example, leaves much unsaid and unexplained as far as people and their needs are concerned, and no one studio course can be expected to reorient students' views of environmental justice and equity, of the criteria for good design, or of the professional's role and responsibilities.

2. Raymond Lifchez and Dana Cuff, "Prologue," *Journal of Architectural Education* 35, no. 1 (Fall 1981): 1. (This is a special issue of the journal, entitled *With People in Mind: The Architect Teacher at Work*, edited by Lifchez and Cuff.)

Good courses and good teachers are important, but more important are good professional schools, schools whose curriculums and policies embody a coherent set of values that speak not only to their students but to society at large. By proposing a vision toward which society should strive, professional schools, like other social institutions, can exert an intellectual and ethical influence beyond their own perimeters.

In this, we were fortunate to find ourselves in Berkeley, a city that has become a mecca for physically disabled people seeking "independent lives," and to work with a department of architecture that has earned a reputation for its concern with social issues. The idea of our teaching experiment was original to us, but Berkeley—the city and the university—provided human resources and intellectual climate that enabled our project to flower. Among our accomplishments, we hope we have strengthened our community's commitment to its human values.

Index

Able-bodied people, negative responses to disabled people: aversion, pity, 15, 115, 150, 168; curiosity, 63, 84, 104, 109, 149; depersonalization, 3, 14, 20, 27, 30, 37–38, 70–71, 113, 150; fear, anxiety, guilt, 6, 14, 65, 88, 129–30, 144–45; fear of offending, 14, 64, 90, 149, 158; view disabled as homogeneous, 6, 14, 64, 85, 90, 149, 150; view disability as technical problem, 64–65, 81–82, 84, 91, 103, 111, 116–17

Access: design criteria and strategies for, 38–40, 41–43, 59, 105, 116–18, 138–41; as perceptual orientation to humanity, 49, 54, 119–21, 185; public policy on, 2; as quality of experience, 33, 40, 59, 105, 117, 119. *See also* Ramps

Accommodation. *See* Client accommodation; Co-ownership of design; Needs assessment

Anecdotal evidence, value of, 16, 44–45, 84, 91–92

Architects: investigatory methods, 45–49; profession's response to disability, 2–3, 37–40, 49–50, 69–70, 81–83, 113; profession's self-image, 113; responsibilities to clients, 32–33, 43–45, 49; responsibilities to society, 5–6, 15, 40, 49–50, 78, 113, 120–21. *See also* Client accommodation; Co-ownership of design

Architectural Design with the Physically Disabled User in Mind project: conflicting agendas, 68, 69, 72–75, 82–83, 132–33, 144; design problems, 55–59; evaluative measures, formal, 56, 59–62, 75–78, 155–60; evaluative